IF
PIGS
COULD
TALK

IF
PIGS
COULD
TALK

BEN GILL

ISBN : 979-8865-16788-4

Interior design by Booknook.biz

*To my friends who actually
believed me when I told them*

"Pigs Really Can Talk"

CONTENTS

PREFACE

I have waited a long, long time to write this book. I will disclose the story behind the title somewhere in the pages ahead, but not quite yet. There are lies to be told, chapters to be written, and sunsets to capture our attention before we get to the pigs. As the words flow from my fingers to the page, there will be a time for revelation, but this is neither the time nor place.

Perhaps this is a good time to introduce myself. My name is Ben Gill, and as we say in Colorado, this is not my first rodeo. I have authored a few books, some of which people actually bought. If memory serves me, of the first six books I penned, "Stumbling Up the Stairway to Heaven" was my best seller of all time. I should have checked the sales numbers before I started writing this, but I think we printed a first edition run of 1500 copies.

Amazon was the publisher; in the last count, we sold 27 copies. We did not sell 27 copies. Six copies went to kinfolks who, I might point out, demanded free copies. One copy went to my hometown newspaper. That one was free too. Subtracting the deadbeats who got free copies, we sold 20 copies. However, if Amazon can be trusted, 11 of those sold would be returned by people demanding their money back.

So let me alert you to one fact right now. No matter what Prince Harry says, this book writing is not the gold mine it is let on to be.

I was born on a farm in Northeast Arkansas, just nine miles from the banks of the Mississippi River. Our farmhouse had no running water or electricity. For the basics of life, we had a freshwater well at the back of the house and a little two-seater outhouse that served other needs.

My Dad died when I was nine months old, so at 24, my Mama became the "lady farmer" who tried to make a living from the Arkansas soil.

The story of how that turned out will be told in the chapters to follow.

The nearest town was four miles away. That would be Dell, Arkansas, with a thriving population of 107 fine Christian folks. Fifty years later, I returned home to bury Mama, only to find the road sign still listing the population as one hundred and seven. One of the old timers explained that the population stayed the same because a man left town every time a baby was born. Hey, that made sense to me.

Dell was a wonderful place to grow up. As boys who were not seeking a gender remodification of some sort, we were free to get dirty, have a black eye, and work when it was harvest time.

In Dell, we had teachers who taught and a doctor who saw to our health, and we did not expect either to cross vocational lines. Fortunately, Randi Weingarten did not set her sights on the teachers in Dell. The teachers were allowed to love, hug, encourage, and educate all thirteen in my senior class without interference.

Life brought me many experiences, but one directly relates to this book. In 2011 my adoring audience encouraged me to write a weekly blog. Three hundred and eight blogs later, I retired for the 15th time. With no weekly blog to write, I sat in my easy chair to enjoy soap operas for the rest of my life. As of today, I have been at this soap opera task for three weeks, and my brain has turned to mush.

Rather than being known as a "mush-brain" for

the rest of my life, I decided to make this compilation of blogs posted during the four years of my peak creativity.

That's correct. You read the previous sentence correctly. This was, without a doubt, my years of peak creativity. By that, I mean this is as good as it gets from this old man's computer-worn fingertips. So don't go buy this book and two months later come running to me asking for a refund. I warned you.

Now back to the title. This farm I was raised on had a plethora of farm animals. We raised dogs, cats, mules, pigs, horses, goats, sheep, ducks, geese, pigeons, and just about anything else that could either be eaten or trained to do a job, such as pulling a plow.

Mama had a story to tell about every animal on our farm, but her most outrageous story related to the pigs. I was just a little kid, and I believed her when she told me pigs could talk. If I told a lie and Mama found out about it, she would say, "I was talking to the pigs this morning, and they told me you lied to me about going to school yesterday."

So, Uncle Red, you will hear about him later, had taught me that the two most powerful words in the English language were "dammit and hell." Therefore, when Mama would say the pigs had ratted me out, my first thought would be, "Damn those pigs." Had I said that out loud, Mama would have given me two black eyes and a broken arm. Mama was not one to hear profanity coming from the mouth of her baby boy.

Besides that, Mama already knew the truth. The damn pigs had been talking again.

I share all of that with you because, in the chapters to follow, there is a strong possibility I will embellish the story a bit. That will be done as either a creative enhancement or I have just started making up stuff to make the story more interesting.

So for you, the reader here is the key. At the point I realize my lightening fast fingers have started enhancing, I will insert the code (IPCT). That will stand for "If Pigs Could Talk," and you will know my sinful fingers have started making stuff up again.

You will be rightfully informed, Mama will be proud of her baby boy for being so honest, and the pigs will be waiting to give Mama the rest of the story.

Finally, there is one other style note that we had better agree on before it becomes an issue. Contrary to all publishing norms of our day and to the chagrin of my editor, there are sections where I will use the conversational style of the wonderful southern Mississippi Delta where I was raised. My buddy, Bobby Johnson[1], went to high school with me and joined me in a search for a Ph.D. Bobby got his degree in astrophysics from MIT or Stanford, one or the other. I got mine from the School of Hard Knocks by paying $25 for the diploma. But that's another story.

The point is that when old Bobby and I get together these days, we both drop back into the language of the South. "What is you doing, big boy?" "You Ain't looking no better than a dead horse in a rainstorm." Well, you get the idea. Just understand that when conversational "Southern" is spoken, education takes second place to down-home communication. As we say, "Just roll with it."

So if you are ready, let's just dive into chapter one. This is the story of Prissy Missy, the cat. I don't think you will find IPCT, but keep your eye on the story. That old code might just jump off the page when you least expect it.

---

1 In most cases where proper names are used, I will just be making up something. I had rather fight legal battles with a fictitious character than a Harvard Ph.D. any day.

CHAPTER ONE

I was twenty years old before I lived in a town with a real live, professional, tax paid for fire department. Until then, my fire protection had come from volunteers who cut hair, changed tires, cooked at the cafe, and did many other things to support themselves. Then when the fire alarm went off, they dropped everything and ran to the firehouse to protect all of us, other citizens, from disaster.

In Dell, Arkansas, there weren't many buildings to catch on fire, so about every six months, Bubba Wilson or Charlie Dodson would get up at midnight and set something on fire so the fire volunteers could get some practice. That worked well until Bubba got drunk and set his own house on fire, but that is another story.

This is not to imply that the fire department in Dell only showed up to work on days or nights when there was smoke in the air. Not at all. These fine men, no females were allowed in the hallowed halls of the Dell Firehouse and Domino Parlor, also served the community in other ways. For instance, they led the Fourth of July Parade in Dell, and that was no small matter.

The whole town only had six streets, and to make the parade last as long as possible, they had to circle around about four times, thus causing havoc on the roads and streets. The parade finally got filled with so many homemade floats that Niza Richardson tried to stop the use of the fire truck. His logic was that with all that traffic, if there ever were a fire in town, the truck would get tied up in traffic, and the building would burn down before the firetruck got to the fire.

Now to my knowledge, the boys never kept a building or house from burning down anyway, so I never really thought it mattered.

The fire department had other uses. During election time, the truck could be used to distribute campaign material. Today that would probably be a problem, but in 1952 if you weren't a Democrat, then someone had been messing with you anyway, so there was little harm in just letting the boys work for Harry Truman on the side.

Also, it was not uncommon for the fire department boys to be called on to rescue some animal, farm, or pet that had become stranded in a tight spot somewhere. If the truth is known, the Dell Volunteer Fire Department was probably at its best in such rescuing situations. Well, I guess you have to put an asterisk on that statement since the tragic events of May 1961.

I left my hometown to go to Texas in 1957, but here is how the story was handed down. It was in 1958 that Mrs. J.O. Dedman-Wilson, daughter of the Russian Revolution (IPCT) and probably sister of Emperor Nero, moved to Dell, Arkansas, from London, England. She had come there to marry J.O Wilson, one of the fine United States of America boys she had met and served with in the big war called World War II. She had met many of our fine young men during the war and, according to rumors, had certainly done her part to serve the rest, if you get my drift.

From the moment she hit Dell, she let everyone know she was a woman of "letters" and had some stock in royalty back in the old country. No one ever saw Mrs. JODW, as she was called behind her back, doing such things as hoeing the garden or picking up crap in her front yard like everyone else. No, sir, this woman of high blood did not do such things.

What she did was give "high teas" about twice a month. If you were invited to such an event, you had to buy a new frock, get your hair done at Judy's Solon and Pet Store and show up with a small gift of appreciation. This was no invitation to be taken lightly.

Let me regress for a moment to say something about Mr. J.O. Wilson. That man loved his woman, and they had not lived in Dell for many years until he had taken on airs just like her. He got to wear his Sunday suit down to the post office each morning, so that ought to tell you something. He tried to get everyone in town to call him "Baron," but that lasted about a week. Then Shorty Collins slipped and called him "Bastard" at church one Sunday, and that sort of took the icing off the cake. Right after that, the Baron went back to being J.O. just as he had been for the past forty-some-odd years.

But anyway, J.O. loved that woman as soon as she got off the boat in Charleston or where ever. Some people said he had a hammer in hand and was building her a fine plantation home before the train could transport her from Charleston to Dell. It was by far the largest home in Dell. It had large plantation columns in front, and the front veranda wrapped completely around the west side of the house. I guess it would be the side veranda.

They had "servant's quarters" out back. That one I never figured out since servants were out of style since around the end of the great war - great war in the South defined by the Stars and Bars - God Bless America!

Old black Minnie and her sister lived out there and were assigned to making the "lady's" every wish come true.

Well, anyway, there came a day when a catastrophic event took place there at the Dedman-Wilson house. Just to get right to it, Mrs. JODW's cat, Missie Prissie, got up in the pecan tree in the front yard and could not get down. They tried everything to get that cat out of that tree, but she simply would not move. Finally, as the day moved toward evening, it was decided to call the Dell Volunteer Fire Department to bring one of their long ladders to the scene. It was time to get serious about that cat.

The call went out, the siren went off, and just like the rapture at the end of time, the volunteers dropped whatever they were doing and headed for the firehouse.

"Where's that far we going too?"

"Ain't no far hits some savage beast lose at J.O.'s house."

With that bit of information, the troops descended on the plantation manor like Patton chasing Rommel across Africa. Within ten minutes, nine of Dell's finest were standing on and around the firetruck as they tried to see the crisis before them. Mrs. JODW was crying into Minnie's shoulder, J.O. was running around giving orders, and the firemen were trying to decide who was going up the ladder to get what had now become known as "that damn cat!"

Finally, one of the new boys was chosen, and up the tree he goes. The cat climbs higher, and the fireman climbs faster. Until in one swift swing of his arm, the fireman has the elusive cat and makes his way down to place the little darling in the arms of his beloved Mrs. J.O. Dedman-Wilson, daughter of the Russian Revolution and probably sister of Emperor Nero. The crowd cheered. All was right with the world. Missie Prissie, God bless her little cat soul, had been saved by the Dell Fire Department.

Sensing a rescue on the horizon, thus seeing a

chance for citified entertainment, Mrs. J.O. Dedman-Wilson instructed Minnie to set up a table of refreshments under the other big tree located about ten yards from the scene of the rescue. A starched white cloth covered the table, and cookies, cakes, and other assortments of goodies were placed there, awaiting the speech J.O. would make in celebration

A bottle of the finest Brute Champaign adorned the table as an added touch.

"I just want to say thank you to all y'all who help rescue my wife's cat.

Miss Prissey is like a member of this family, and y'all done saved her life. Y'all are mighty fine folks, and I want you to share in a little cake and drink in honor of this wonderful occasion. As a token of my appreciation, I will give this new $50 bill to the fireman's fund. Thank y'all, and drink up."

The celebration began, and Mrs. J.O. Dedman-Wilson is so overcome with emotion that she decides she must say a word or two. Placing the rescued family pet on the grass, she walks over to the table and makes a few remarks.

She talks about the Fatherland and some other places no one had ever heard of, and before they knew it, a celebration was in force. Finally, people are hugging and associating together in such a way that one would think a Baptist revival was going on.

With the celebration over, the firemen begin to load the ladder back on the 1947 Ford Fireball fire truck. Everything all squared away, the firemen waved to all, and with the siren blaring, they rolled down the driveway on their way home from another victory.

And promptly ran over and killed Miss Prissey!

Lord, help us all.

CHAPTER TWO

Are you as tired as I am of our lack of civility today? Frankly, I am about fed up with how my fellow humans act. My goodness, some congressman actually shouted out in the middle of one of President Obama's[2] speeches last year, "YOUR LYING!" Well, maybe he was, or maybe he wasn't, but there was a day when no one of proper upbringing would

---

2 This is the first use of a President's name. From this point forward, when writing about any President, I will not use the real name. I will just refer to "the President." I do that because I am going to say some pretty tacky things about Obama, Bush, Trump, Biden, and a bunch of others. By not using their real name, I will not know what party is trying to "get" me for bad-mouthing their beloved one. I did not learn to do this in journalism class. I learned it from having been shot at twice after making some harebrained remark about Clinton a few years ago.

do such a despicable thing. We were just nicer back then.

And what about all these people running around in Egypt last week? Of course, I think they should have an opportunity to speak their mind – either for or against the government – but do they have to beat the reporters over the head with stones just because they are doing their jobs? I don't think so. I really don't. Maybe everyone could just lighten up a little bit.

Many years ago, I bought a little house and 40 acres of land out in east Texas. It was going to be a family weekend getaway. Having been raised on a farm, I thought I probably knew everything there was to know about planting a garden and living off the land.

My first mistake was trying to break up the land for planting by using a garden tiller. That east Texas gumbo soil just wrapped those little tiller blades up in knots. It took about two minutes for me to realize it was going to take more power than I had to get that land ready for planting.

The second mistake was trying to do all this preparation on a day when the Texas heat was hitting around 110 degrees. Something told me I might be about six weeks too late. Maybe planting should be done in the spring. Well, while I was making these two enormous discoveries, I looked up, and the neighbor up the road was coming across my field on his tractor. I might add that the tractor had a big plow on the back. He drove up, and the conversation went like this:

Charlie: Well, I see your trying to plow up yo're garden. How's it coming?

Me: Not too good. What do you think?

Charlie: I guess I thank hell is going to freeze over before you get it done with that tiller.

Me: Yea, probably right. What about that plow on your tractor? Think I could get you to plow up this garden for me?

Charlie: Yea, probably could.

ME: What do you think you would charge me to just hit that spot once or twice with your plow?

Charlie: (Looking at me like I had kicked him in the mouth) Well, son, if you will let me "neighbor" you, I'll plow it fer you fer nothing. But you need to know I don't hire out.

So he neighbored me and plowed it up for nothing. Yes, sir, I liked it back when people were nice, and I wonder why it can't be that way again.

About six months ago, I was boarding a plane in Vail to fly to Dallas. I had been bumped up to first class, and I was just standing around reading a book when they announced first-class boarding. This young guy behind me reached out and pushed me aside, and ran ahead to board the plane.

Well, as luck would have it, I found him seated next to me when I boarded.

I said, "Wow, you were in a hurry back there. What was that all about?"

He looked at me with a (let's call it a smirk) and said, "Well, I just rolled over three million miles on American, and they sort of like for us top travelers to board first."

I had been waiting for this guy for years. I opened my briefcase, pulled out my current mileage card, and said, "Don't have my glasses on. Just got this thing in the mail last week with my current mileage number. What does it say?"

"Nineteen million miles!"

"Yep, they sort of like us to be nice."

As we look at this coming week, what if we all lighten up a little bit? Pick out one person and say something nice to them. Do a good deed for someone without them knowing who did it. Open the door, pull out the chair, smile, you know, the drill. And then ask yourself:

WHAT DOES IT TAKE TO BE NICE IN THIS WORLD?

CHAPTER THREE

What is the most important thing in your life? No, seriously, how would you answer that question if you were forced to answer it? Obviously, some would immediately say "family," and others might say "friends." A few might mention a "thing" or perhaps others a "cause." But I want you to consider the fact that how we answer this question is not as important as how we live the answer.

I have a friend who, for a number of years, was a professor of Evangelism at Southwestern Baptist Theological Seminary in Ft. Worth, TX. Here was a man whose teaching responsibility was to help young seminarians answer that question. In every lecture for every class, he taught them to say that Christ was the most important thing in their life. Day in and day out that was his message.

When I first met Ken, he was a young professor, moving to the top of his career, and he was unmarried. Within the first year of our friendship, he met and married a lovely young lady. In the marriage, he got a wonderful, beautiful young bride who wanted very much to please her new husband. What she got was a college professor who was set in his ways, had lived alone all his adult life, and someone who knew exactly how he wanted things run. He was particularly exacting concerning the white shirts he wore on a daily basis.

After a few months of marriage, his young wife decided to save money by washing and ironing his shirts rather than sending them out to the laundry as he had done in his single life. Well, as Ken describes it, her efforts were a disaster. Buttons were missing, and collars were starched in the wrong place - anything that could go wrong did. Something had to be done.

So one evening after dinner, he said to her, "You know honey, I think you are working too hard. You always seem tired, and I want us to do something about that. Let's look at some things we can have others do around the house so that you do not have to work as much. You know, like doing my shirts. I know that takes a lot of time, so what if we go back to sending them out? I am really missing our time together."

She agreed, and the deal was struck, and the next week he sent his shirts back to the shop that had laundered them when he was single. Three-day turn-around, and early on the third day, he was there when they opened to pick them up.

Later that day, as they were getting ready to go out to a seminary function, he began to put his shirts in his closet when he noticed that all the shirts, every last one, have been ironed with pleats down the front. Which would have been wonderful, except none of his shirts were pleated.

Angry was not the word! He was livid. Here he had finagled to get his wife to agree to send his shirts out, and now every last one was ironed wrong. And worst of all, he was going to have to wear one of these now pleated shirts out to dinner.

The next morning he stormed down to the laundry and threw all the shirts on the counter. Before the very young and pregnant woman at the counter could say a word, he pounced: "Why couldn't they get his shirts right? Who was the idiot who wrote up the order? Was everyone so stupid they could not see these shirts were not pleated in the first place?"

According to his own description, he was pretty much the poster boy for an angry customer. With one final swing of his arm, he threw the shirts across the counter and told the clerk he expected them to be ready by five. BANG! He had made his point!

Fast forward ahead about two months. Ken and his wife were members of a Baptist Church in Ft. Worth, and the church leadership had decided to visit all the families in their area of Ft. Worth who had a baby born in the previous month. Ken and his wife attended the "Baby Night" dinner to be assigned a family to visit. Ken's heart stopped when they were given the card with their assignment. There on the card was the name of the young woman from the cleaners. The very one where he had blown his top about two months earlier because his shirts were not done correctly.

He didn't tell his wife about the incident. He also didn't sleep much at all that night. Morning came, and he was still in a quandary. What should he do? How could he call on this young family when he had treated her so badly at her place of work?

Later that morning, he called his secretary and laid out the entire problem for her. His question to her: "OK, you see the problem I have. What do you think I should do?"

With no hesitation, she replied, "I think you should take that card back and let someone else visit them. You see, I know her. Her name is Norma, and she and her husband are friends of ours. And frankly, Dr. Chafin, after that incident, she doesn't think the most important thing in your life is Christ. She thinks the most important thing in your life is shirts."

Oops! So I repeat. When we are asked what the most important thing in our life is, the most important thing is not how we answer the question, but it is how we live the answer.

If every night, the last thing our child hears us say is, "I told you to get in bed, and I mean it. NOW GO TO BED RIGHT NOW, AND DON'T GET UP!" Do you think the kid might get the idea that the most important thing in your life is bedtime?

If we come home from work every day and the first thing they hear us say is, "Leave me alone. I need some time to myself. Get out of here." You think they might think the most important thing in our life is time away from them.

Go on and make your own lists. You know what things you focus on with your actions, even if they don't match the words you say. Write them down. Look them over. Now answer the question: What is the most important thing in your life?

Interesting, isn't it?

CHAPTER FOUR

The Lord came to me last night and sat right here on the corner of my desk and said to me, 'Sam, this is what I want this church to do. I

want them to build a mighty sanctuary, and I
want you to lead them all the way." And then the
Lord just got up, shook my hand, winked at me,
and walked out of the room. It was a wondrous
experience to know exactly His will for us."

Southern Baptist Pastor
Large Church in Alabama
Building Committee Meeting

"Gill, what did you think of our pastor?"
"Seems like a nice guy," I said.
"Crazy as a loon but a preaching machine. It
would be great if we could lock him up all
week and let him out on Sunday to preach."

Chair of the Building Committee
Same Church

I'm sorry, but I have to admit to you that I have
never actually, like in an audible way, heard the voice
of God. I did hear an actor at the Passion Play up in
Siloam Springs, Ark., one time speak over a micro-
phone like he was speaking the words of God, but
he sort of talked with a lisp, and it just didn't sound
right to me.

When I was growing up in Dell, AR., we had
a deacon who would occasionally hear from God,

and maybe it was because I was just a teenager, but most of the time, I just didn't believe him. One year the Methodists were planning on having a big dance in their fellowship hall, and they invited the Baptist kids. Mr. Densmore got up in church the next Sunday and said that he had heard straight from God that the Baptist kids ought not to go to that "hellhole" down at the Methodist church. He said that God had told him we ought not to go because all that dancing would lead to "Lord knows what" after the "juices of gender had been aroused."

Well, I, for one, wasn't going anyway because I had just broken up with Sara Johnson. But when I found out that the juices of gender might get aroused down at the Methodist church, I immediately let it be known I would be there. Unfortunately, nothing happened, so we just assumed that Mr. Densmore had gotten the message wrong.

Maybe it was the Episcopal church where the real things were happening, but by then, we had already wasted a night with the Methodist.

But my point is that I sometimes get a little leery of someone who runs his or her business by just listening to the voice of God. I just think there is a real possibility they might get the wrong message and be in a heap of trouble.

Two of our companies raised money for nonprofit organizations. That included churches, hospitals, universities, and all kinds of worthwhile causes.

Some years ago, I got a call from the head of one of these fine organizations saying he needed to raise about $1,000,000 to do this great work. I will admit it was a worthy cause and needed to be funded. As we talked a bit further, I said that I would have our people submit a proposal to his board in order to authorize our work. (IPCT)

There was a long pause on the phone. Finally, "Wait a minute," he cried, "you are going to charge us to raise that million?"

"Yes, that's the way we make our living. We are a fundraising company, and we do charge a fee for our services."

"Well, how much is it going to cost?" There had suddenly entered a rather stoniness to the conversation.

"I don't know at this point, but you should expect your program expenses to run in the range of 3 percent to 5 percent of the dollars raised." I thought that was pretty good when the national average at the time was closer to 20 percent.

But all he heard was the 3 percent to 5 percent, and with a tone of total dismay, he said, "But Ben, God told me to call you folks, and you would do it for free."

Without skipping a beat, I quickly replied, "Exactly what time did God tell you that?"

Now with desperation creeping in, he said, "Last night when I was praying just before going to bed."

I'm sorry, Lord because I know it wasn't very nice, but I just couldn't pass it by. With sadness, I said, "Oh, that explains it. You see when I was praying this morning, He told me you would call and not to get suckered into thinking He had told you that I would raise your money for free."

He then broke down laughing and said, "Gill, you got me there. Send us a proposal, and let's get to work." Over the next few years, his organization became one of our better clients.

I tell you, folks, I just don't think we should play around with the "God told me" stuff. I believe God leads, inspires, guides, touches our intuition, speaks to us through His Word, and directs us in a multitude of ways, but I just get a little leery when someone catches Him on tape giving the directions.

Stay with me because I am going to get to the personal and business application to this "thought" in a minute, but for now, I just want to share one more example. Many years ago, a well-known national religious leader visited our office. It was a big day for us, and so we all dressed in our finest and tried to talk in "thee and thou" type language.

Mom was still with us, and when I told her who was coming to our office, she immediately informed me that she was going to be there to see him. So on the appointed day, we plopped Mom down in her wheelchair and headed for the office. No sooner had we gotten Mom seated among the group when the great leader arrived. We welcomed him and listened while he said a few words of inspiration to our staff. I do not diminish the importance of that moment. His words were encouraging to all our people who support the work of our consultants.

Then as he starts to walk away, he sees my mother. With the room very quiet, he walks over to Mom, kneels down, and takes her hand. He says a few private words to this aged saint, and then he asks Mom just one question, "Mrs. Hardin, is Ben your only son?" Touched by the moment and with tears in her eyes, Mom reports that I am her only child. With that question answered, the Great One rises to walk with me back to my office.

As we go down the hall, he says with deep sincerity, "Ben, I know you wonder why I asked your mother whether or not you were an only child. You see, I had to affirm something. This morning while I was preparing for this moment, God told me that I would be meeting your mother, and then in a voice as clear as a mountain sky, He said to me, "Be kind to Ben, for he is her only child."

"It has always been like that in my life. Every morning I get up, and God tells me a new fact about the day ahead. That was my fact today, and I just had to affirm that I was still hearing the voice of God."

Now, folks, I'll just have to tell you I didn't know what to say. There was a strong possibility I was in the presence of a saint. Here was a person who actually heard God talking out loud that very morning!

There was only one thing that gave me pause. I didn't have the heart to tell him that I had a brother. Mom had just forgotten about him in the excitement of the moment, so for that moment, I was an only child, just as "God had told him."

Now, the thought came to me as I remembered that event. Each of us must be very careful when we make our life decisions. We must be careful of the voices we listen to and follow. We must be careful of our business decisions and the counselors we listen to as we make those decisions.

It has been my experience that if I check my decisions against:

- His Holy Word
- Knowledgable Counselors
- My intuition
- His standard of values as set forth in the Word
- The test of integrity
- and a measure of common sense

then the decisions I make will have been made under His leadership. I'm a bit leery of voices. But I have great confidence in His Spirit within me directing my ways.

There is a difference.

CHAPTER FIVE

This morning in the mountains, a slow rain is falling, a thin fog covers the mountains at about 8500', and clouds cover the sky. Our home sits at 8175', so the fog covers us like a canopy in the jungle. As I sit on the balcony, one simple thought comes to mind: it was a long road from there to here.

"There" began on a hot August day in 1957 when my dad took me to the Trailways bus depot in Blytheville, AR, to take a bus to Texas to a University I had never seen. As he hugged me, he placed a lone $100 bill in my hand and said, "Son, I hope this will help. We will try to send more if we can." My journey had begun.

Prior to this day, my life had been no different from a thousand other farm kids in the Mississippi Delta. From about six to twelve years of age, I was a "water boy" carrying drinking water to the field workers who chopped cotton under the hot sun. At about twelve, I was given a hoe to use in my eight to ten-hour day chopping the weeds from the cotton rows. Today I guess we would call it child labor.

When the day was over, I went home to a house with no running water and an outhouse. When I was about ten, we got running water and indoor fixtures. The shower head was still on the outside wall facing north. Cold water only – summer and winter. This was the life I was leaving on that hot August day with my $100 stake for the future.

In Texas, I worked two to four jobs at a time and graduated in five years. Then it was on to seminary, where I worked three jobs but got a graduate degree in three years. As life moved on, I started a company and hopefully made a contribution to the world. And then one day retired. On my last day at work, I logged over 25 million miles on American Airlines, averaged about 200 nights a year in a hotel room for about 30 years, and put together the finest group of fundraising consultants ever assembled in one organization.

I had no student loans, small business loans, or other financial support during that time. It was to go to work each day, grow when we could, and retrench when we had to. It was a crazy, fragile life, and all in all, it was a typical life in America.

So on this foggy morning, I reflected on the "from there to here." "There" is a bus station in Arkansas. "Here" is the balcony on a home in the mountains of Colorado.

This opportunity came to me because my great-grandfather had chosen to come to this country from Ireland in the late 1800s. He disembarked his ship in NY with his stake of $100 (maybe it was $10 back then). He journeyed to Arkansas and made a life for his family by clearing land and claiming a homestead. It was a hard and often frightening journey, but he did it to make a better life for his family. And he made that journey within the confines of the laws of his adopted country.

As the beneficiary of his courage and labor, I stand today as a proud American.

Here is the lesson from the balcony: I wish every citizen of every other country in the world the same opportunity. Come to America. Bring your dreams for your future and plant them in the soil of this great land. We welcome you, but that welcome comes with one condition. When you come to this country, come within the framework of our laws and respect our structure. Those who do will have the same opportunity for success as that twelve-year-old kid in Arkansas. Fail to respect this country, and you should be sent home.

It is not a matter of race, social standing, skin color, or the language you speak. It is a matter of right and wrong, legal and illegal, or law-keeper or law-breaker.

Come and respect our laws, and you can focus your life on building your future. Anything less than that, and you will spend your life in the shadows of America, fearing the authorities.

And such it is and such it should be.

CHAPTER SIX

I have always considered myself a patient person. I can stand in long lines without going ballistic because someone is hoarding the time of those who are waiting to be served. I can endure long sermons even when the minister made his point long ago, and it is now evident he is only filling time. Yes, I have always considered myself a calm and patient person. That is until today.

Today I met the misnamed "customer service" division of the RingADing phone company. Five hours after that first meeting, with only one thirty-minute break, I am still trying to get my problem solved. I have been transferred to six different departments, told to go to an on-site retail store which I did, and also was told to "hold." I have been dropped twice, and my problem is still unresolved five hours later.

(Update – one week later, with 24 hours of phone time, the problem is finally resolved. RingADing had been billing our wireless to another person, and that person wasn't paying. So if you have been paying my wireless bill for the past few months, please keep paying. When you stopped, you greatly complicated my life.)

About 20 hours into this RingADing experience, I gave in and admitted the world had won. I acknowledge it. I am no longer a patient person.

Today I am giving in. From this point forward, I am going to rant and rave, shout when I have to, talk loud enough for everyone in line to hear me, and tell the customer service representative that they are incompetent and that my pet pig could do a better job.

Today I surrender. (IPCT) I give up, give in and walk away. Being nice just doesn't cut it anymore. And this life transition took no reading from a Holy Book, no voices from the heavens, nothing like that at all. It simply took 24 hours on the phone or holding on the phone with RingADing.

Wow! Do I feel better already!

So now you know the new me. I will look back at this week and re-think how I handled some situations.

Last night my wife and I walked down to a local neighborhood restaurant. It was a beautiful early evening dinner, so we asked to be seated on the patio. After sitting there a few minutes, a couple of women at the next table started talking to us, and before we knew it, the evening was flying by. Early twilight, no wind stirring, and new friends at a neighborhood restaurant: what could possibly ruin this wonderful experience?

Smoke! Two tables over were two women who, about midway through the evening, jump-started their cigarettes and started, in unison, to blow their smoke our way. We are not talking about a little smoke. We are talking about enough that some other diners were about to call 911. Did they smoke just one? Oh, no, they were lighting one off the other before long. Anyone within twenty feet would surely have smoked-filled hair, smoke-smelling clothes, and a beautiful dinner ruined.

So how did I handle it using my old persona? First, I commented to our new friends that our dinner was about to be ruined by a couple of smokestacks at the second table to our right. Then I coughed a few times and waved my hands in such as way as to make them seen by everyone else in the room. And the best part was that after making a scene, I was able to leave the restaurant quietly and then complain to my wife all the way home.

But no more! The next time I am confronted with such a situation, I am going to follow the example set by a fellow traveler I once sat by on an American flight from Chicago. This was before the Democratic idiots were elected and ran the city into the ground. I have made a vow. I no longer will travel to any city where one's safety is only guaranteed by the length of the gun they take with them.

But back to the story. We were in a three across row seating, and the gentleman on the opposite side of my companion said to him, "Do you mind if I smoke?"

With no hesitation, my friend said, "Of course not. Do you mind if I fart?"

Case closed – that is the type of tactfulness I plan to use in the future. No more Mr. Nice Guy for me.

Actually, (IPCT) if I carry this new attitude forward in my life, I resolve a lot of "how do you handle this" issue questions. Now when I am going to be late, I don't have to apologize to anyone; I can just say, "To hell with you. I arrive on my time – not yours."

In business, I can promise anything and deliver nothing. That seems to be working for the government, so why shouldn't I incorporate it into my lifestyle?

At dinner parties, if the food is not up to snuff, I can just say in a loud voice to anyone listening, "That may have been the worst meal I have had this year."

Why shouldn't I be that open with my thoughts and feelings?

It is almost as if the dumbing down of America has gone from the area of intelligent knowledge to the ways of everyday living. Last week I heard a CNN commentator talking about the tragedy that happened on the "Continent of Japan." With that level of ignorance, why shouldn't I drop to the lowest common denominator in how I react to and interact with others? Why should I let her remark pass instead of buying a billboard and plastering the city with a sign that says, "You dim-wit! Japan is not a continent."

I trust you see where I am going with this. In each of our lives, there are hundreds of events each year that we can react to in the old socially acceptable ways, or we can pull out the stops and make a fool of ourselves while making certain everyone within earshot hears us complain.

Yep, I think I am going with the latter approach from now on.

(Long pause, deep breath)

Well, maybe not. For some reason, it just doesn't fit me. It doesn't feel good. Sure, it had a momentary high of satisfaction, but I know that when I go to bed tonight, I am not going to feel good about myself.

So I guess tomorrow I will go about standing in line and not complaining to some little customer service representative who has no power to help me. When the woman blows smoke my way, I will probably just get up and move to another table without making a scene.

Why? Maybe because I had rather be nice than first. I would rather be known for my contribution and not the scene I cause. Etc, etc.

But I tell you one thing – it sure did feel good for a minute.

CHAPTER SEVEN

OK, here is the BIG one.

I am going to introduce you to my Uncle Red. He is no longer alive, but when he was, he lived life to the fullest. As a little kid, I saw him as bigger than life. And then I grew up and realized that the amazing thing about Uncle Red was that he REALLY WAS bigger than life. He was one of those characters who sometimes come in and out of our lives, and life is better for the experience.

Uncle Red enjoyed a taste of the vine on occasion. He was never one to drink alone. He was the type who would buy the entire bar a drink. Keep in mind that the fact that he had no money to pay for the bar tab was just a minor part of the story. Everyone loved Uncle Red.

His legend grew in our family until often, when

thousands of miles away from our roots, we would find ourselves calling back to someone in the family to ask, "What has Red done recently." And then, from the voice a thousand miles away, our family spy would burst into laughter and tell the latest Uncle Red story.

Sometimes even today, when the cares of this world seem too burdensome to carry, I will sit in my office with the lights down low, a diet drink in my hand, and let the memories of this funny old uncle take me to a time when life was less litigious, and people were a bit more kind.

It was Sunday, April 10, 2011, and Red had been gone for a week. Our little town of fewer than 125 people in northeast Arkansas knew something was wrong, but they had been there before. Every once in a while, when the cares of the world got to him, Uncle Red would just get in his car and drive away.

Those of us who were kids at the time never knew the real story because the adults would talk among themselves in conspiratorial whispers behind closed doors. The only thing the younger group knew for sure was that Uncle Red was gone again and that Aunt Eva was growing angrier by the day.

Dear Aunt Eva was a saint if ever there was one. Uncle Red stood about six feet tall – Aunt Eva was 4'10. He weighed about 220 – on her best day, she might weigh eighty-five pounds. But that little lady could move that big hunk around with a look or a word so stern that Uncle Red would be like putty in her hands. And when Uncle Red disappeared as he did from time to time, there was always one thing he would know for

sure. Every day it would become harder for him to return because he knew he would have to face Aunt Eva. This time was not unlike the previous ones. He had been gone for a week doing Lord knows what, and Eva was ready for the kill as she awaited his return.

As fortune would have it, my cousin Jimmy and I were in front of Mr. CA's country store on the day Uncle Red returned home. Now sober, remorseful, and fearful of coming back home, Uncle Red drove up to where Jimmy and I sat on our bikes:

"You boy's doing awe-rite?"

"Yes, sir, we doing just fine. How 'bout you?"

"Hell, I'm doing awe-rite, but I may not before long. Y'all seen your Aunt Eva?"

"Yes sir, she's over to y'alls house, and she's really mad at you, Uncle Red. Don't think I would go home right now."

"Yea…"

He got out of the car and walked around a bit. You could tell he is really thinking things over. He knows he is in big trouble.

He looks at the pay phone hanging on the wall by Mr. CA's front door. He is muttering under his breath, but we can't make out what he is saying, "Now Eva, I been down to Memphis on biddness and…"

He stopped and walked back. He acts like that's not coming out like he wants it to.

He is walking and mumbling, and you can tell he is trying to figure it out. All of a sudden, he claps his hands, jumps in the air, and runs to the pay phone. He is fumbling in his pocket for the required dime needed to make a call.

"You boys, come here. (IPCT) Either one of you

got a dime I can have?" Uncle Red never had any money of his own.

Jimmy digs in his pocket and gets his last dime, and gives it to Uncle Red, who is so excited he almost drops it before he can deposit it in the phone. Finally, he puts it in the coin slot and dials his own number. He looks at us with a glow on his face that lets us know he has everything under control.

Listening hard, we hear Aunt Eva answer the phone, and the moment she is on the line, Uncle Red yells into the phone as loud as he can,

"Eva, thank you, Jesus, Eva is that you? Lord knows I am glad I got to you in time. EVA, DON'T PAY THE RAN-SOME – I GOT FREE!!!!!!!!!!!!!!

Those were good years, and they hold great memories. Most of us long for the day when life was easier and less complicated. Do you remember:

- Leaving home and not locking your door.
- Playing Kick the Can with all the kids in the neighborhood
- When pay phones were a dime.

- When there were pay phones
- TV's were black and white, and the networks closed at midnight with the playing of the national anthem
- Elvis
- When guys rolled up the cuffs on their jeans
- Your girlfriend had to be home at 10:00 because her parents CARED about her.
- Teachers knew your name
- Bikes had only one speed, and in almost every family, there was an Uncle Red.

These moments of nostalgia were brought to you today by a guy sitting in his office with the lights down low and a Diet Pepsi in his hand.

Thanks, Uncle Red, for the wonderful memories.

CHAPTER EIGHT

It is Thursday morning, and I am preparing my weekly blog. The focus this week is obviously on weddings since tomorrow is the big day for William and Kate. I advise you that I am writing this on the day before the wedding because if something unexpected happens tomorrow, I want you to know I did not know it at the time of this posting. If Kate forgets her lines, some idiot blows up a trash can, a rock goes through the window of the carriage, or the present Queen refuses to attend, at this moment, I do not know about it.

I just want to reflect on weddings.

If my history has taught me anything, it is that a wedding or a funeral is an open game for unexpected events. Anything can happen and usually does.

The undertaker in a small, county-seat town in

Texas called a friend of mine to officiate at the funeral of a stranger. In his defense, my friend had neither seen nor heard of the family who sat before him on that sad day.

The family gathered in the chapel, awaiting the minister to begin the service. Soon a door opened behind the altar, and the minister walked to the pulpit, and the service began.

"We are in this place today to pay homage to this great woman who was the backbone of this family."

A voice came from the congregation. "It was Papa."

Not hearing the whisper from the pew, the minister continued. "This great woman was the jewel of this family, and God loves a life such as this."

A bit louder, "It was Papa!"

Still not understanding, "The Bible says that a woman like this is of more value than gold or silver."

Finally, standing up in the third row, one of the family members shouted, "Look in the box, you idiot. It is Papa!"

Yes, unexpected things can happen at public family events. But we must move on to weddings. There is something about a wedding that can bring out the occasion's beauty or something unexpected that can be the unwanted focal point of the event for years to come.

But no place is this more problematic than at a formal wedding. Rings can be lost, and vows are often forgotten, bride's maids can faint, or, as seen on one occasion, the best man can have a heart attack. We can just pray that none of these happenings take place at the Royal wedding in London tomorrow.

Unfortunately, a problem-free wedding was not to be the case in First Baptist Church, Walton, Texas, those many years ago. I will try to the best of my ability to relate the events of that memorable day, but you must read this very carefully lest you become totally confused.

As often happens, the minister had served the congregation long enough to have seen many of the children grow into adulthood.

One day they were playing in the church nursery, and a brief time later, they were walking down the aisle to be married.

On this day, Ann, the mayor's daughter, was married to Sam. Sam was not a hometown lad and had only been introduced to the minister at the rehearsal dinner the evening before the wedding. Everyone thought they made a beautiful couple: this daughter of the town and this stranger from Dallas who had won her hand.

Actually, the fact that she had chosen Sam was a great surprise to many. From their early childhood years through middle school, high school, and the first year of college, Ann had been fondly linked to John, son of the local football coach. They were a couple. People kidded them about being married and having children, and coming back to the community to raise their new family. It was to be a fairy tale marriage for this small Texas town.

But a strange thing happened. Ann and John had gone to the University (if you are not from Texas, this refers to the University of Texas. If you are from Texas, no explanation is needed). They came home for Thanksgiving and Christmas, still a couple. They came home for Spring break, still a couple.

But on May 1st, word comes that Ann was engaged to this stranger from Dallas. The wedding would be on June 14th at the First Baptist Church, with the family minister officiating. The town was shocked, abuzz, and expectant. This is a wedding no one will miss.

It is Saturday afternoon at 4:10 pm, and the organ plays. The wedding party has made its way to the front of the church, where candles light the altar for this joyous ceremony.

The bride enters on the arm of her father, a proud man who looks over the congregation and thinks of the one hundred grand he is spending to make this a special day for his daughter. One look into her eyes, and he knows it is worth every penny.

With every person in place, the minister begins the ritual of marriage. He reads I Corinthians 13. He talks of the unending circle of the ring and the unblemished metal from which it is formed. And then he comes to the repeating of the vows. This may not be exactly how it went; some said later that it was much worse. But let me attempt to replay it for you.

Minister

Do you, Ann, take John to be your lawfully wedded husband?

Voice of Bride's Father from the second pew (a whisper)

It's Sam.

Minister

Do you, John, take...

A louder voice from the second pew

It's Sam!!

Minister (a bit flustered)

I'm so sorry. John, would you take...

Very Loud Voice from Man Standing at Second Pew Very red-faced. Fuming.

It is Sam, you sorry son of a bitch!!!!!

Some said the minister left town that night. Years later, others said he had gone to the Sunday morning service the next morning to apologize for his mistake that seemed to have ruined the perfect day. But all agreed that on that Sunday morning, as he gave his resignation speech, he tried to make amends by saying,

"I just want to apologize to the Martin family for my mistakes yesterday. And I especially want Ann and John to know how I wish them a long and happy life.

I said what?"

"You said, John again."

"Whatever."

CHAPTER NINE

She was an old lady, and one day in March, almost twenty years ago, she died. It was not a glamorous death. The family was not all sitting around telling old funny stories about the family while she just drifted off. No, that's not the way it happened at all.

She was in a nursing home and had been in a coma for about three weeks. Her sister, Peggy, had come from the East Coast to help out. Holly and I had been with Mom around the clock for all these many weeks. Ron, a grandson, had flown in from Tokyo when he realized his Dad needed his support. Dee, a granddaughter in London, called every day to make certain we were "holding up," as we say in Texas. Lucretia, another granddaughter who lived nearby, came from time to time.

We liked to think Mom was aware that we were

there, but she probably wasn't. Death has a way of closing the senses and bleeding the soul while at the same time making those who attend the ritual feel needed and wanted. They probably aren't.

On the night she died, only Peggy was there by her side. Holly and I had gone to get a shower and eat another greasy hamburger from McDonald's. Ron had gone home to Tokyo the day before, having used all his vacation time to be with Granny and to give his support to Dad. When we got out of the car at the home, Peggy met us in the driveway with a simple, "Bert died about five minutes ago."

And with that simple statement, it was over. One life, 82 years, two sons, 39 years in a little green house in Dell, AR., and six wonderful years with her family in Dallas, and then a miserable three weeks of dying, and it was over. It is amazing how complex and yet how simple life can be.

What this story is about is the six years in Dallas and the three weeks in the home. The story is a two-sided coin, the meaning of which can be seen on both sides. I will choose to focus on the joyous one, but the message is probably on the other side.

Mom lived in Dell, AR, population 107, with me gone. Dell had a school that her kids attended, a church where they got "saved, sanctified, and set apart," and memories. After open-heart surgery and falls that left her with two broken arms, Holly and I went to Dell one January morning and told Mom it was time to come to Dallas and live with us. She shed a quiet tear, looked around the home she had shared with PaPa for all those years, and said, "Well, if it is time to go, let's do it." That afternoon we helped her pack a bag. Less than six hours later, she started her new life in Dallas.

The process began with a physical exam by her new doctor. He took her off most of her medication and gave her some vitamins. Within two weeks, she was ready to hit the road. And for the next six years, that is exactly what she did. We took her to London! She had never been out of the States.

We took her to see relatives and friends. We had long weekend trips in the country. My Episcopalian wife took her to a Baptist Church, and when Mom became too fragile to leave the nursing home to go to church, Holly went with her to the nursing home service and sang off-key with all the other geriatrics.

We took her to the zoo and almost lost her when we turned to look at the lions, only to realize we had not locked the wheels on her chair. While our back was turned, she zoomed down the hill at full speed laughing all the way. In London, she held her first great-granddaughter. At the Texas State Fair, she ate her first Fletcher's Corn Dog. In Paradise, TX, she ate at a real live bunkhouse. It was a glorious six years.

Then came the three weeks – the other side of the story.

For the last three weeks of Mom's life, she was pretty much in a coma. Life was playing out, and all the rituals of death were surrounding her. A fine young doctor helped her to remain at ease through the process. Shifts of nurses were always there just to let us know they cared. I wish I could remember their names, for they brought honor to their profession.

Over the three weeks, we became accustomed to the professionals coming and going. A blood pressure check here or a pill there. In and out, always pleasant, never intrusive.

But there was one who seemed a bit out of place. Each day around 3 o'clock, she would walk into the room, walk over to the bed, look down at this sleeping tiny little person, and say, "How are you doing, Mrs. Hardin? Is everything going okay today?" Receiving no answer, she would look at the family member who might be there and say, "Well, I'll check in tomorrow," and she would leave.

Day after day, the ritual went on. No one from the family asked about this woman. We were busy caring for and loving the sleeping, tiny little person who never answered.

For three weeks, the process continued until, on the day before Mom died, I said to this unknown phantom of the nursing home, "Who are you? Do you work for the Care Center? You have been very nice to come by, but what do you do?"

You are not going to believe this, but without blinking an eye, she replied, "Oh, I am the occupational therapist assigned to work with Mrs. Hardin."

"Occupational therapist!" I cried, "What the hell are you trying to do? Teach her to type!"

Indignantly, she responded, "Well, when she gets better, we certainly want to make certain she can take care of herself, don't we?" We checked the billing sent to us later, and sure enough, there it was.

Those little drop-in visits by the occupational therapist had been billed for three weeks at $35 per day.

Then we looked further and found a speech therapist that came by each day and billed $35 per day for her visits as well. We assume Mom would be ready to "testify" at church about her miraculous cure had she come out of the coma. After all, someone thought she had been blessed with a speech lesson each day.

But there was a lesson learned, and I learned it. Please allow me to share it with you just as I learned it in the midst of this terribly sad experience. I learned that my job and your job should have value. It should have integrity. It should be necessary. What a tragedy to go to work every day with the conscious intent to do nothing of value. Occasionally we should ask ourselves if our world is better for what we do or if we just fill space and collect the pay.

As I was coming home from work today, I saw a man standing on a road repair site, flagging traffic. All day long, he stood there and kept the cars from running into one another. My guess is he was uneducated, probably making minimum wage, but his job had dignity and value.

Our momentary visitors at the home had education and a look of professionalism. No doubt, there were many others who needed their services. But in our case, it was evident from the first week that the ritual of death was taking place in this room. So, in this case, they had no value. They were taking up space in a room where an old woman was dying.

Look at your job today. Does it have dignity? Does it have value? Is humankind better off for what you do? If not, you might want to call the Texas Highway Department. I understand there is a shortage of people who hold the flag to keep the cars from crashing into one another. The job requires no education, and it doesn't pay very much. All it really requires is integrity.

I want to close by acknowledging the benefit therapist of many types can bring to a situation. When I had bypass surgery, I was immensely grateful for the therapist who taught me how to put my shirt on. Otherwise, I might still be bare-chested when I go to work or church.

But someday, when I am dying, I pray that the same therapist will be around to comfort my family without trying to make the visit just another billable hour.

CHAPTER TEN

He was sixteen years old. I did not know him, but over the years, my family told his story, and I would listen, and I would learn. I would listen to the stories about his relationship with his father and how they fought. Not figuratively, they fought with fists and sticks and words. It was a sad, soul-destroying relationship, and one day Billy could take it no more. I would learn how important sixteen years can be in a young boy's life.

His older brother Jiggs had already walked away, leaving behind the "bad blood" of the family. Now it was Billy's time. He was sixteen, and the family was at war, but so was the country.

Hitler's troops were storming, and by most accounts received here at home, the German army was winning, mile-by-mile and country-by-country. Here in the States, we went on ration cards for everything from fuel to meat. School children had scrap drives where every metal object found, new or old, could be donated to the cause. Pots and pans were melted down to make tanks and trucks. Families planted Victory Gardens to grow food for the nation. The world was at war.

Billy slammed the door and walked away from home. He went to the recruiter's office at the county courthouse and signed up for the Army. He was not big for his age. He had skinny little arms and legs. He was only five feet six inches tall. Who knows, maybe he weighed 130 pounds. He was a little guy, and he was only sixteen years old.

The recruiting officer explained to him that he was about ten months early. At this point in the war, you had to be seventeen to sign up. Billy was sixteen plus two months. He had walked away from home ten months too early.

Oh, there was a way, the sergeant informed him. "Get your daddy to give his permission, and if he will sign with you, we have just the spot for you." As he turned to leave, the sergeant gave him a few pages to be filled out. On top of the stack was the permission slip he needed to have signed.

Billy probably thought that would be the end of the journey. He left the courthouse and went to a friend's house to stay for a few days. Each day there, he listened to the radio and longed to be in Europe fighting. Mostly he wanted to be anywhere but home.

It was a Sunday afternoon when he finally went back home. Calling out to his mom, he soon found himself in her motherly embrace. Her tears flowed that day. One son had already left to go live in California. He would never come home again. Lord only knows where Billy might be if he had not come home that Sunday. She held him tight lest he also disappears.

A few minutes later, he is sitting under the willow tree out back. He had seen his father out there sitting alone and thought he might be able to have a civil talk with the old man. No one seems to know what was said, but a few minutes later, they walked back to the house. The old man called for his wife, and when she came in, his only words were, "Kiss your baby boy goodbye. He's gonna be saving us from them Nazis." Derision in his voice and posture.

Any news from Billy came from the few cards and letters he sent to his older sister, Bertha. Maybe an occasional note to Peggy, the baby of the family, came every few months. Not long letters or informative notes. Just "They sent me to the Army Air Corp, so maybe I am going to fly a plane or something."

"I am off to train with my crew. Can't tell you where I am, but, but looks like I am going to be out of the country for a while." A postcard with every sentence of the message redacted by the military censors except "…tail gunner in a B-17 Flying Fortress."

No, no! Not a tail gunner. Could there be any worse job in the Corps than that of a tail gunner on a B-17? The tail gunner had to sit in his "bubble" at the very rear of the plane. Temperatures in the bubble were usually sub-zero: his seat was a bicycle seat. He would "ride the seat" for missions lasting up to several hours while bumping and bouncing along at 30,000'.

In the early days of the Fortress, he would almost always be the first one in the crosshairs of those German pilots who so wanted to blast this Allied bombing factory out of the sky.

His mother prayed, "Dear God, please keep Billy safe. And dear God, please don't let him be a tail gunner. Anything but that, dear God."

If his father prayed, no one heard him. If he cared, he didn't show it.

I have tried to put a year on it, and with proper

research no doubt I could. I think I must have been either four or five years old when on a very cold winter night, my mother took my brother and me to spend the night with Granny.

Thinking back to that evening, I have two vivid memories: first came the memory of a soldier in uniform knocking on the door and then the scream coming from the lips of my grandmother as she realized why he was there. The second memory is one of the family standing around a potbelly coal-fired stove in the middle of the living room.

"This telegram just says he is missing in action. Maybe he's still alive."

"They don't send any army sergeant to people like us if he ain't really dead."

"He was so young. He was so, so young."

Billy was still sixteen when he was shot down over Germany. He just never made it to seventeen. A couple of years after the war, we got a letter from the War Department letting the family know that Billy was indeed killed in action while serving as a tail gunner on a B-17 Flying Fortress somewhere in Germany.

What were you doing when you were sixteen? My memories take me to the municipal swimming pool in Blytheville, Arkansas, where I would spend an afternoon debating whether or not Elvis was the greatest singer ever to live. Sixteen was probably the first taste of true love. Sixteen was taking that love to the drive-in and trying to make our parents think we were going to see the movie.

Sixteen was senior high, graduation, planning for college, and trying to decide whether I wanted to be a hippy or not. Sixteen was an A in algebra, and having my heart broken by that girl, the one I took to the movies and plans and dreams unfolding for the life ahead.

Sixteen was a very good year.

But not for Billy. For Billy, sixteen was fighting at home, going to war, kissing his mom goodbye, freezing on a bicycle seat at 30,000', and trying not to get shot in the bubble. For, Billy, sixteen, was hearing the captain yell, "We've been hit. Bail out! Bail out!" and knowing that once the plane started to fall, there was no way out for the tail gunner.

In WW II, there were 405,399 Billys. "We are sorry to inform you that your son (father, brother, sister, daughter) was killed in action."

In that same war, 670,846 were wounded.

The average age was twenty-two.

Maybe that is why I get upset when our schools no longer recite the Pledge of Allegiance.

Maybe that is why I get livid when I hear General Milley, Chairman of the Joint Chiefs, getting so protective of the woke agenda. Maybe that is why I say don't kick good soldiers out of the military because they don't take a Covid shot.

Maybe that is why I get upset when our leaders, from the current president down, try to negate religion from our society.

That is why I get livid when Sec of the Navy, Carlos Del Toro, budgets money for a recruiting campaign that features drag shows with dancing drag queens. If you want to know how to make a recruiting video, call Tom Cruise, for goodness' sake.

Maybe that is why this summer, while we are watching the ballgame or firing up the grill, it would be appropriate for us to pause for a moment. Maybe that is why somewhere on this ship we call America; it would behoove each of us to remember the men and women who made this country possible. They fought for us in world wars. Some died in Korea, and others in Vietnam. Let's not forget the "minor wars" and the Gulf wars, and then there is Iraq and Afghanistan.

All who died to give us this freedom are heroes of the nation. All who were wounded and maimed deserve our respect as the flag goes by and the national anthem is played.

And let us not forget.

Some of these heroes were only sixteen.

CHAPTER ELEVEN

A few years ago, our company had a contract to raise funds for a church in Nashville, TN. One of my dearest friends, Jon Pirtle, was assigned the job, and for several months he pretty much lived in Nashville. This was like going to heaven for Jon because he was a big country music fan.

I wish you could have known Jon Pirtle. Jon was a tall, white-haired country gentleman, and when he laughed, he turned as red as a stop-light. So, of course, those of us who worked with him tried in every way we could to give him something to laugh about. Those were fun years.

But, anyway, Jon had been assigned to this church as their fundraising consultant, and when he had been working for them for a few days, he realized that most of the country music stars living in Nashville were members of this church. Jon was elated. Here he was getting to do a job he loved with people whose careers he had followed as a country music fan.

Week after week, he would come back to the Dallas office and tell us whom he had met, whose house he had dined in, what star he had enlisted to work in the campaign, etc. This man was really living his dream.

On one trip back to the home office, I asked Jon why he had to spend so many weekends in Nashville.

Of course, I knew the answer – he was going to the Grand Ole Opry on Saturday nights as a guest of the Opry stars. Once I found that out, I immediately started to finagle an invitation. Within weeks Jon had an invitation for Holly and me to attend the Opry as a guest of Mr. Opry himself, Roy Acuff.

To many of you, this would not be a big deal, but for an old country boy from Arkansas, this was about as good as it would ever get. You see, I was raised on country music. In fact, when I was about thirteen, my stepdad bought a new AM/FM radio, tuned the tuner to WSM-Nashville, Tennessee – radio home of the Grand Ole Opry, and then he took the knobs off. If it couldn't be heard on WSM, it wasn't worth hearing.

A few years later, Roy Acuff ran for governor of Tennessee, and my daddy threatened to move our entire family from Arkansas to Tennessee- see just to live under the protection of "our" governor, Mr. Acuff. Of course, when candidate Roy Acuff didn't win the election, my daddy declared he would never live in a state with voters as ignorant as "them dim wits in Tennessee."

But I digress. So Jon had gotten us tickets to the Opry as guests of Roy Acuff. Finally, the weekend arrived for us to go to the Grand Ole Opry, not at Ryman Auditorium in downtown Nashville where the Opry had originated, but in the new auditorium on the grounds of Opryland. I bought a new pair of jeans, brushed off my Western hat, put on my boots, and headed to Nashville. Life was good!

Jon and his wife, Pat, were waiting for us when we got to the auditorium that Saturday night. Jon was walking on air because the four of us had been invited back to Roy Acuff's dressing room. This was heady stuff for two old country boys and their "little darlings."

Roy Acuff could not have been nicer. He invited us into his dressing room, a room somewhat smaller than our house in Dallas but not a lot smaller. The walls were covered with pictures of the legends of country music. And before we knew it, the walls came alive as country star after country star came by the dressing room to pay homage to Roy Acuff and to meet his guests for the evening.

The first black member of the Opry, Charley Pride, stopped by, and we talked about his upbringing in Sledge, Mississippi, where he was one of eleven children. In 1967 Charley won a Grammy Award for Song of the Year for the hit "Just Between You and

Me." But it was not until 1971 that he won Entertainer of the Year for his biggest hit, "Kiss an Angel Good Morning." Up until that time, his picture was never on an album cover because it was thought a black entertainer could never make it in country music.

I liked Charley Pride, and after talking with him a bit, I think he liked me. Thank you, WSM Radio - Nashville, TN.

Sarah Ophelia Colley Cannon stuck her head in to say hello to Roy, and as would be expected of a country gentleman, he introduced us to this fifty-year legend of the Opry. Oh, you may know her better as Minnie Pearle.

And on and on, the evening flew by. Reba McEntire, a star who would go on to sell over 51 million albums worldwide, starred at the Opry that night. The Statler Brothers did their thing.................. WOW!

And then it was over. The evening moved on, and it was time for Roy to go back to his home built right there on the Opryland grounds. And it was time for our party to go back to our hotel, catch the plane the next day and return to our homes in Dallas. Memories of a lifetime had been built within this little circle of old and new friends. It was a time to remember, and there were stories to tell for years to come.

Roy Acuff died not long after that night. Opryland would later be sold to the Gaylord Broadcasting Company of Oklahoma City, and then a few years later, the entire project was demolished, and the scene of our memories would be gone forever.

Jon passed away from cancer sometime after that night. When Jon died, I lost more than a friend. I lost someone who could talk country music with me until the sun came up and someone who would always make me feel ten feet high when he complimented me.

In 2005 I sold our company, the company where so many of us had spent our entire business careers as we tried to raise money for God's work around the world. Within two years, our 35-year legacy would just be a mirage of a past well lived.

My wife and I moved to Colorado on a part-time basis. Other members of our firm are scattered around the world. Times changed. We changed. But each of us had our own personal memories of nights in Nashville to fill our thoughts and bring joy to our hearts.

I guess the message this week is just to remind you that everything you do in life cannot simply be a way to make a living. Oh, that is certainly a worthy goal, but that is not everything there is to life. Sometimes each of us needs a "night in Nashville," a special weekend at the newest hotel in town, or even a night that we have made special because we have special people in our life.

So I urge you to make some memories this week. There may come a day when all the physical attributes have gone away, but a well-lived memory is a joy to remember forever.

CHAPTER TWELVE

One morning last week, I was driving down the Dallas tollway listening to the top news of the day. Another tornado had hit Joplin, MO., the mighty Mississippi was flooding, and Donald Trump was in another fight with the press. But the story that almost made me pull over to the curb and cry was the news that Bob Dylan was 80 years old. Lord, help us all! If Dylan can live to 80, the rest of us ought to be able to pass a hundred like a witch on a stick.

Old reclusive Dylan is 80. Can you believe that? It seems like only yesterday he was singing his poetry in the bars of San Francisco as the crowd gazed through the smoke to see if the cops were going to take us down. Old Dylan is 80.

The Big 80!

And Elvis is dead. Some people remember where they were when President Kennedy was killed. Me, I remember where I was when Elvis died. Elvis of the *Blue Suede Shoes* and living in the *House of the Rising Sun*. Elvis with his pink Cadillac, powder in the spoon, and a Mansion on the Hilltop. That Elvis was bigger than life and deader than a doornail. Yep, I remember where I was when he died.

Of course, some would remember Janis Joplin's overdose with a bottle of Southern Comfort at her side or Rickie Nelson's plane crash over east Texas on December 26, 1985. It seemed at the time like James Dean hitting the only tree on the road to Paso Robles, CA. would earn a place as a national day of mourning.

I guess everyone remembers what is important to them. And I remember all these dates like a second-hand computer. Can you believe it? Old Dylan is 80, and "Yazoo Street Scandal" and "Hard Rain Falling" are still in my top ten.

Isn't life funny? You live thousands of days, and then from time to time, something happens that just nails that date in your memory forever.

Let me challenge you to do something today. Take a few minutes and write down ten special days in your life and, specifically, what happened on those days that locked them in your memory. You may not know the exact date, but do a little work this week and see if you can find the specific date for each one.

I think of my list, and though I don't plan on sharing them all with you, I see these dates as an overview of my life from 30,000 feet. Some dates are personal family matters, and others are national events we all lived through. OK, so I will share a few with you even knowing I am going to miss something really important.

Of course, four of my ten would have to be the births of each of my four grandchildren. Is it a shame that we have to wait until we are so old to have grandkids? In our case, we have one granddaughter and three grandsons, and the day these little kids came into my life, everything else seemed insignificant. That is not to exclude our daughter and son, but grandchildren do take it up a notch.

What about 9/11? Did that day make your list? I was speaking at a convention in Atlanta and was right in the middle of my speech when the announcement was made that the towers in New York had been hit.

Of course, the speech was canceled on the spot, and I will bet you that no one in the audience put that day on their "important day" list because of my speech. But I bet it is there for other reasons.

December 10, 1996, I was flying on American Airlines from Chicago to Dallas. Just as we reached altitude, the captain came on and announced that we had lost one of our two engines. In fact, the one failed engine was on fire, and the fire suppressant system was not working. Somewhere around 37,000', we were on fire.

We were told of the situation and informed that we would be "diving to land" in St. Louis. I looked out the window and could see the flames from the engine. A second announcement was made, and we were told to take the brace position – one way or the other, we would be on the ground in about four minutes. I didn't know whether the brace position was to keep us safe or to help us kiss our ass goodbye, but along with sixty-five other passengers, I complied.

With fire engines parked on each side of the runway, our pilot made a perfect landing. Suddenly we were hit with foam, and almost immediately, we evacuated the plane. No explosion, no injuries, and no headlines. But that date is deep in my memory bank even today.

On May 6, 2001, I was confirmed into the Christian faith. Prior to that, I had played a role that took me through college, seminary, and the position of senior pastor of a Baptist church. Long before that date, I had served as a very top-level executive in the largest Protestant religious denomination in the world. By that May 6th date in 2001,

I was the CEO of a company working with churches. But a few months prior to this confirmation service, I had walked into an Episcopal Church in Plano, TX, and for the first time in my life, actually committed my life to Christ. And then confirmation and a date that is firmly ingrained in my being.

Now your important dates may not be like those at all, but make your own list and see what you learn about yourself. And once that list is complete, I ask you to do one more thing. Look into the future and ask yourself, "If I could make one more memorable day, what would I do that would last in my memory forever?"

Maybe you would save that day to do something for someone else that would change a day in their life. Maybe it would be a day to get things right with

God in your own life. I do not know what your day "eleven" could be or will be, but I do know that you have an opportunity to have a memorable experience.

And best of all, you get to choose what that memory will hold.

P.S. Just a word of advice: If at all possible, I would stay away from airplanes with burning engines.

CHAPTER THIRTEEN

In this chapter, I am going to share a story with you that is not at all the way I planned to open this chapter. When I wrote the first draft of this chapter, and frankly, the more I wrote, the more disgusted I became with the whole bunch of us.

At the time I wrote this first draft, I was looking at a beautiful hi-rise building in Dallas that was under siege by a bunch of Black Lives Matter commandos who were attacking our street. For many years my wife and I had lived in this building. But tonight, when we came back from a vacation, we found the building surrounded by a razor-wire barrier. Our co-op Board of Directors employed five armed guards to help keep the residents safe. We were cautioned not to take our dog for a walk after dark until we could schedule an armed guard to accompany us.

We lived on the 15th floor, so we could see what was taking place around us. A Target store just across the freeway from us was being raided by an out-of-control mob that carried BLM protest signs. Cars on the street in front of our building were stoned with prepositioned bricks.

It was reported that the situation became so out of control that two black children were killed by the rioting mob. And this mob was on the march in one of the safest cities in America. This was not Detriot or Chicago. This was Dallas, where people felt safe walking the street alone at night. This was Dallas, where I had lived since 1975.

What caused things to boil over into mass confusion and danger?

Now for the rest of the story. A story that began in a sharecropper's house in rural Arkansas. What is a sharecropper's house?[8] Here is a picture of one just like the one where I entered this world in 1939.

This is what is called a "shotgun house." It had a front door into the living room. A middle door into a bedroom and a third door into the kitchen. The back door opened into the backyard. A person could stand on the front porch, shoot a shotgun in the front door and have the shot go completely through all three rooms, and exit the back door without hitting a single thing. Thus the name, shotgun house. There was no running water. The facilities were in an "outhouse" in the backyard. We would get electricity when I was about five years old.

About a quarter mile up the dirt road in front of our house, there was another shotgun house exactly like ours. Henry and Mary Ann Jones lived in that house with their six children. Their young-

est son was my age. His name was James, but we called him Danny.

When Danny was about ten years old, his father loaded up all the family in the family car and drove the fourteen miles to Blytheville, the nearest town of any size. After a day of shopping, Henry rounded up his family to make the short drive back home.

At the same time Henry was doing that, a big eighteen-wheeler was entering the same highway carrying a full load of oil pipes. No one knew the car full of the Jones family and the unknown driver of the big rig would soon meet nose-to-nose at a combined speed of eighty miles an hour.

In a matter of minutes, police arrived to survey the wreckage. Ambulances were called. More than one would be needed. On that early spring day when the sun was high in the sky, a tragedy took place on that road leading the Jones family home. When the casualty count was taken, Henry and four of the children were dead. Only Mary Ann, Olivia, and Danny remained.

If anything, the bonds of friendship between Danny and me grew stronger over the next few years. Both of us were growing up without a father in the house. So our high school years, when we dreamed our dreams together, we did so without a father figure. So supportive of each other, we moved forward in life.

Finally, there came a time when I would leave for Baylor. I left for Baylor and never came home again except to visit with family.

Danny left home and went to college somewhere in Arkansas. The last time I saw him was at my mother's funeral. At that time, I think he was the Superintendent of Schools in Little Rock. Seeing him at such an emotional time in my life, it is possible I have his position wrong, but the point is that he had made a great life.

He had made his way without a father or, as is so often said, "No man in the house." He had made his way after an education reading used books handed down from a richer school. He had made his way the same way I did. He worked his butt off to pay his own way through college.

And each of us did it with "no safe place" provided by the universities we attended. He never threw a brick, set a building on fire, or shot at someone he didn't like. And he was a good kid, just like I was a good kid. And we each turned out ok.

By the way, have I mentioned that Danny was black? Mary Ann used to laugh at me when I was about four or five years old because I would look at the palms of her hands and say, "Mary Ann, your hands are dirty." And they would all laugh at me because I didn't know what black hands looked like. No one ever thought of filing a lawsuit.

Now I look out over the street where Black Lives Matter is holding a march about something. And I find myself saying, "Dear God, what has happened to us?"

Twice this week, the President has encouraged a much-needed dialogue between white and black America. His contention is that our two worlds are so totally different that meaningful understanding between the two is almost impossible. That is without "meaningful dialogue."

For once, I agree with the President. Perhaps our only difference on this matter is the nature of the dialogue. Based on other statements by the President, it would seem his idea of dialogue is for white America to listen to black America.

I agree that is necessary, but the difference comes from where this discussion stands today.

I would contend that Black America has been shouting, protesting, rioting, and preaching its points for years. The missing piece, in my opinion, is the message from White America. Whites have been intimidated for years because when a valid point is made against Black America, the one making that point is most often vilified as a racist.

Well, I think it is time for someone to speak up for White America. Wow, I never thought I would use that term. For most of my adult life, people have referred to Black America. Among the social boundaries of our day, that was acceptable.

"Black America wants justice."

"Black America wants reparations for past injustices."

"Black America is upset."

"Black America will march in 100 cities next Saturday."

And on and on you could go. For seeming generations, Black America has pushed its agenda everywhere, from the streets to the classroom. The rallying cry from Black America has basically been "We want, we want, we want."

Just today, our president said, "We need a dialogue. We need a conversation about race in America." Well, Mr. President, maybe someone will direct you to this blog because this white boy is about to speak out for White America. Call it black bashing or anything else you want, but I, for one, think it is about time someone spoke for the other side. I am sad the two sides have to be separated like this, but your head has been in a hole somewhere if you do not recognize the black/white division in America today.

Rev. Jeremiah Wright was President Obama's pastor when he was a community organizer in Chicago. He officiated the wedding ceremony for Barack and Michelle. President Obama and Rev. Wright were good friends, and many of the writings by the president were influenced by Rev. Wright.

And then, one Sunday, the President's friend preached a sermon that would change things. September 11 was still in the hearts and minds of Americans everywhere when the right Rev. Jeremiah Wright preached a sermon where his true colors came out.

"And the United States of America government, when it came to treating her citizens of Indian descent fairly, she failed. She put them on reservations. When it came to treating her citizens of

Japanese descent fairly, she failed. She put them in internment prison camps. When it came to treating her citizens of African descent fairly, America failed. She put them in chains, the government put them in slave quarters, put them on auction blocks, put them in cotton fields, put them in inferior schools, put them in substandard housing, put them in scientific experiments, put them in the lowest paying jobs, put them outside the equal protection of the law, kept them out of their racist bastions of higher education and locked them into positions of hopelessness and helplessness. The government gives them the drugs, builds bigger prisons, passes a three-strike law, and then wants us to sing "God Bless America." **No, no, no, not God Bless America. God damn America** *— that's in the Bible — for killing innocent people.* **God damn America** *for treating our citizens as less than human.* **God damn America**, *as long as she tries to act like she is God and she is supreme. The United States government has failed the vast majority of its citizens of African descent*

News commentators around the world spoke on the issues brought up in Rev. Wright's sermon, but one, most agreed summed it up. Pat Buchanan, the speech writer for Richard Nixon and Communications Director for Ronald Reagan, wrote, "America has been the best country on earth for black folks. It was here that 600,000 black people, brought from Africa in slave ships, grew into a community of 40 million, were introduced to Christian salvation, and reached the greatest levels of freedom and prosperity blacks have ever known...

Jeremiah Wright ought to go down on his knees and thank God he is an American."

This nation, from its lowest citizen to its highest offices, has bent over backward to lift up black people to help them succeed. My stepfather was one of the lowest citizens. With a third-grade education, this dirt farmer in Arkansas sent 20 or more black children to college.

He paid for that by the toil of his back in the hot cotton fields of Arkansas. This was in the late 1950s when it was not popular to lift black people up in the South. At his funeral, black doctors, dentists, accountants, and teachers came back from all across America to honor this humble man for his support and encouragement.

This nation, like no other nation on earth, has placed a great focus on black people to help them succeed. Welfare programs, food stamps, rent supplements, Medicaid, legal services, Section 8 housing, and hundreds of other programs have drained the economic wealth of this nation to assist black America in the goal of making black America effective.

Dear people, 611,000 white soldiers died in the great Civil War to free black people. In the great dialogue, how can this be ignored?

And what do we hear in return? We hear grievances and shouts in the street. We hear Al Sharpton and Jesse Jackson on TV raving and ranting about the poor black community. While they stay in four-star hotels and fly first class from place to place to stir up "their community," many children of black America continue in poverty.

Al and Jesse, we hear your relentless bickering about America. But just once, is it possible to express a little gratitude?

But they cry, "We haven't been given a chance to succeed." BS! If you think you haven't been given a chance in life, let me put you in contact with Danny. He will tell you from his own experience what one has to do to get a "chance to succeed."

While black leaders have been indoctrinating their youth into the "gimme" culture, Asian families have been emigrating from Asian poverty into nothing more than the promise of America, and they seem to be able to succeed. Why do first-generation Asians seem to be able to start successful businesses, speak proper English and get off the dole and become productive citizens when some tenth-generation blacks can't seem to do anything but hold their hand out for the next freebie?

A few weeks ago, I talked with an Indian woman who had come to America from India in 2005. She has three children. Last month one graduated from SMU with a law degree. A second daughter was a junior honor student at Texas A&M. Her son was in high school, working two part-time jobs and planning to attend SMU in two years.

I ask this mother how she did it. She said that when she came to the US, she had enough money for about 18 months of living expenses. She said she had worked ironing folk's clothes, cleaning floors, and cooking for rich people. She wasn't complaining. She was thanking America for giving her the opportunity to see her children succeed.

For the sake of sanity, if the Asians can succeed and the Indians can succeed, then why the heck can't black families succeed? And don't tell me it is because they haven't had a chance.

My mother was as white as the driven snow, but she got up at 5:00 AM to pick cotton in NE Arkansas. She sacked soybeans from the top level of a monster combine. And she whipped my sorry butt if I even thought of missing school.

(Disclaimer – save your comments. I know you cannot lump all Blacks, Whites, Asians, and Indians into great generalizations, but you have to be sleeping in that cave I mentioned previously if you don't see the point I am making.)

American leadership has even tried to discriminate against white people to give black people a better chance at success. We tried Affirmative Action. We set aside contracts and quotas to advance minority applicants over white applicants.

Literally millions and millions of dollars have been donated by white and black Americans, and millions of volunteer service hours have been donated to help black America. And what do we get back? We have heard the bickering now: now, can we just hear one word of thanks?

I thought not!

Mr. President, you said, "If you are black, you are more likely to be followed in a store."

Ever wonder if there is a reason for that? Could it be the fact that crime and incarceration rates for African-Americans are seven times that of White, Asian, and Indian Americans? Whose fault is it that illegitimacy in the African-American community is higher than in any other demographic? Is it the fault of white people that the black drop-out rate from high schools in some parts of America is now almost 6%?

Get a life, people! It is time to stop blaming everyone else in America and take a look at your own community. Stop raising kids to get pregnant at 14. Start teaching your youth to talk the same way successful Americans talk. Put a curse on the rap singers who are degrading your children and making fun of their shortcomings. Start taking responsibility for your children instead of expecting everyone else in America to raise them.

Mr. President - you want a dialogue, then let's have one. But this time, give White America the opportunity to say how we see things without then labeling us as bigots. **If the truth is known, the best thing that could happen to White America is for Black America to succeed.**

I cringe every time I hear us divide the country by black or white. But reality says this is where we are today. So what do we do about it?

As an 84-year-old white man who started out in a sharecropper's shack in rural America, my debt to an equal society has been paid. But standing in my place when I am no longer in this world will be another white American.

Or, perhaps it will be another black kid named Danny who raises a voice of reason. Maybe it will be another white student who takes a year out of their life to raise up those who need a chance. We can only imagine who it will be.

But my earnest prayer is that it not be another black student throwing bricks and raising hell. Heaven forbid, let it not be some angry white boy who knows nothing about the world but has now turned to bottle bombs to support some unknown cause.

Both races have their idiot crowds. Let's stop promoting them and start encouraging and supporting those who want to make a positive contribution to themselves and to America.

I'll tell you what let's do. I'll stop listening to white demagogues on the right if you will stop listening to black rabble-rousers on the left. We may be able to right this ship if we work together.

CHAPTER FOURTEEN

I have always been a fan of the Stars and Stripes. In my day, as we old folks are prone to say, we stood in front of our little flag pole every school morning to raise the flag. We fought over who would send old glory up the flagpole. And then, we would sing the National Anthem while holding our hands over our hearts.

This blog was posted on July 02, 2014. The Fourth of July was just around the corner. The bands were tuning up, and the cheerleaders were prancing and dancing. We were about to celebrate America, and what a celebration it would be.

On Friday, July 11, 2014, Holly and I went to the American Airlines Center in Dallas, where we joined 19,000+ fans of Neil Diamond for an evening of music. Picture this as the warm-up band had finished their set when suddenly, there was a joyous vibe felt across the arena.

Unfurling as a backdrop to the main stage was the largest American flag I have ever seen. The lights were focused on the red, white, and blue like never before. This flag would put to shame every automobile dealership in the city of Dallas.

And then Diamond belted out the first notes of "Coming to America." Just typing this, I get goosebumps.

He was not singing about swimming the river at our southern border. He was not singing about paying the cartel $5000 for an illegal ride past the overworked border guards. No, he was singing about the Irish, the Jews, and the countless other nationalities who paid their last dollar to a ship captain who was coming to America.

He was singing about my great-great-grandfather, who tied all his possessions in a tiny sack and made his way to Ellis Island. Diamond was singing about those poor and ragged future Americans who looked up at Lady Liberty with tears in their eyes. They had made it to America, and the promise of America gave them hope.

They came from the shores of Europe and the

sands of Africa. And they came ready to make it to and into America by following the laws of this new land. Here was a country that needed people, and waving the red, white, and blue, the people came to America.

And now, 200-plus years later, we, the sons and daughters of those who came, are sitting in a massive arena with tears in our eyes because someone in our past made it to America. Say it again, "We are coming to America." Say it again and again and again. Black, white, brown, yellow, and gray - they are coming to America.

Let me tell you about the celebration we enjoyed last week. We were singing the songs of America because someone in our past made it to America! They made it to America, and the nation celebrated on the 4th of July

Wasn't this past week a great celebration? All across America, people came out to march in parades, play in bands, watch the fireworks, and, best of all, FLY THE FLAG.

I love living in Dallas because one of the trademarks of the city is the flying of gigantic American flags across the city. These flags will bring tears to your eyes and an extra beat to your heart. God bless this flag and the national qualities for which it stands.

On the 4th of July this year, our family was in Avon, CO, and it seemed the entire village turned out for the celebration. Avon has the largest fireworks display in CO, and this year no forest fires were set from the fireworks show. Up here, we count that as a successful event. We had a picnic, went to an outdoor symphony concert, and played a little golf. The hot dogs were tasty, and the beverages were refreshing. And the greatest thrill of all was we flew the flag.

In the home I grew up in, we had flags.

We had a German flag my uncle brought back at the end of World War II. We never displayed that flag, but every once in a while, Mom would take it out of the drawer, and Uncle Bob would come over and tell stories of fighting in the big war. And when the stories were told, my Dad would take out the American flag, and as a family, we would stand and pledge allegiance to the flag of the United States of America.

We had a Japanese flag that a friend who fought in the Pacific found and brought back for my Dad. The Rising Sun was placed in the same drawer as the German flag. I suppose this was sort of our "enemies drawer," for lack of a better term. As I have studied history, I am amazed we could fight two wars on two separate fronts and win them both. But I am more amazed at how many veterans have pointed out the mighty resolve that poured forth on the battlefield when Old Glory was raised to point the way.

Oh, say, can you see by the dawn's early light
What so proudly we hailed at
the twilight's last gleaming?
Whose broad stripes and bright stars,
thru the perilous fight,
O'er the ramparts we watched
were so gallantly streaming?
And the rocket's red glare,
the bombs bursting in air,
Gave proof through the night that
our flag was still there.
Oh, say, does that star-spangled
banner yet wave
O'er the land of the free and
the home of the brave?

Those are the words we sing as we honor the flag and what it stands for. Those are sacred words where I was born and raised. I don't want to see some want-to-be "artist" trying to show off when they sing it. I don't appreciate Rosanna Barr making a joke of it when given the honor of singing it. You don't show out when you sing "AmazingGrace," so don't act like an idiot when you sing about this "star-spangled banner."

I am having to force myself not to make a political statement as I close this posting. It is not easy because I think present leadership has no idea what this flag represents. And I fear, oh yes, I fear, that my grandchildren and someday great-grandchildren may one day

The Star Spangled Banner

stand before this flag and have no idea of the sacrifice others made on their behalf.

I fear they will stand before that flag and feel no emotion nor shed a tear. And that will be such a sad day for America.

So until that day, let's fly the flag. Not just on

the 4th of July but every day. And for generations to come, may it fly over "the land of the free and the home of the brave."

CHAPTER FIFTEEN

Ok, it is time to lighten things up a bit. I am a long-lasting Arkansas transplant who, in 1957, moved to Texas to attend Baylor University. It took me five full-time jobs and five shots at freshman English to finally get a degree, but by that time, I was an adopted son of the Lone Star State.

During those early years, I spent four years in Tennessee, but those don't count. I got back to Texas as fast as I could. You gotta love Texas. Good, Lord, Willie Nelson was born in Texas. Lyle Lovett was born in Texas. George Bush, the one who was better than a standup comic, was born in Texas. I just wish someone had kidnapped my Momma and brought her to Texas to give birth to me. I could have been one of the wild and famous.

Once a year, the *Texas Monthly,* one of the once

finest magazines in the US of A, publishes a list of reasons people love the Lone Star State.

Take a look at some of the 2014 notable actions:

- **A hummingbird that had flown off course on its migration south was taken by airplane from Minnesota to Texas, where it was released into the wild.**

- **A Woodlands house with a three-story closet was put on the market for $12.9 million.**

- **Fathers at Lakewood Elementary School raised money to buy a car for the long-time crossing guard, whose vehicle had been repossessed following his wife's costly illness**

- **It was once a great Texas monthly magazine, but then the Woke crowd got their hands on it. Now it is just a propaganda rag trying to push a far-left agenda. Get out the dogs, boys. They may be badly needed.**

- **A dog that went missing in the Netherlands months earlier was found near Katy, TX, and returned to its owner.**

Someone said the dog protested having to leave Texas but had to go home anyway.

- An Odessa oil field worker posted a Craigslist ad searching for a homeless woman under the age of 25 who would be interested in living with him and, among other things, cooking, cleaning, playing video games, and engaging in "bedroom fun."

- Two Houston teenagers were arrested after trying to steal a car but first demanding that the owner show them how to operate a stick shift.

- Texas was ranked the twentieth-most-braggadocious state by the travel app *He Lets*.

- After a turkey smashed through the windshield of a big rig passing outside Abilene on Thanksgiving Day, the driver gave the bird to a nearby family for that evening's dinner.

- An Austin man claimed that the face of Jesus could be seen in the burn mark of a tortilla.

Thanks to this month's **Texas Monthly** for reminding us why we love Texas so much. I came to Texas to go to Baylor and never made enough money to go home. Lived here 30 years before I saw the first bumper sticker that read:

I'm Not from Texas
But I got here as quick as I could

I mean, you got to love a state where the Speaker of the House was speaking at an event honoring disabled Texans. Gib Lewis (Democrat, by the way) was never much good as a politician, but he was so goof prone we kept electing him, just for the laughs. So at this event, about 100 people in wheelchairs were lined up at the front of the State House, and when Gib had finished his fine speech, he loudly proclaimed to the honored guest,

We're so proud of our guests today.
Y'all stand up and be recognized!

Yes, sir, you gotta love a state that will elect someone like that to be Speaker of the House.

I was hosting an event at our church one time,

and I had planned to call on Bro. Pevine Ramsay to close in prayer. As I rolled into the final moments, I heard coming out of my mouth,

Bro. Prayvine,
would you lead us as we pee?

Move over, Gibb, here I come!

Yes, sir, I love this state. We have goofy governors (remember Opps!), crazy want-to-be governors (remember "Well, it's like a woman being raped. If you can't stop it, you might as well lay back and enjoy it.") to our credit, we didn't elect that nut!

But it is fun living here. No income tax, low unemployment, semi-good sports teams, and the Dallas Cowboy Cheerleaders. Lord, if I don't make it to heaven, just send me to Texas.

For all you folks who have to live somewhere else. Well, bless your heart, and if you get a chance, y'all come on down. Ya, hear!

P.S. If Texas was listed as only the "**twentieth-most-braggadocious state by the travel app *He Lets,*"** then some of you folks are not doing your job.

Let's get with it! Y'll got that?

CHAPTER SIXTEEN

I have never had sympathy for anyone who would lie to me. When I was in business, everyone employed in our company knew that the unpardonable sin was "to lie to Ben." Everything else might be negotiable, but that one character fault was not covered. Thousands of times, I have said, "If you lie to me or lie to a client, you will be gone before the sun goes down."

It seems to have worked because I can remember only once or twice confronting a situation where dishonesty was a problem. But in those few instances, I was a man of my word. Step back and listen for the door to slam!

I am convinced my obsession on that point came from having a Momma who would beat the living hell out of my brother or me if we lied to her. I must confess that after a few trips to the woodshed, that little Christian lady had made a believer out of me.

It was not until much later in life that I finally learned there was a difference between lying and being just plain stupid. Starting out as a "boy preacher" in the back woods of Arkansas, I was anything but a Biblical scholar. One of my first sermons, at the tender age of 15, was to be on Noah and the whale. I waxed elegant for about 25 minutes, quoting scripture and waving my hands in the air about good old Noah going down to Nineveh and getting swallowed up by that great fish.

After the sermon, the little old ladies came by to say how wonderful my sermon was and how it had touched their hearts. I was basking in sinful praise until a little six-year-old girl said loud enough to be heard in the next county, "Preacher, wasn't that Jonah and the whale instead of Noah?"

Listen carefully. That hiss is the air going out of the High Reverend's ego.

To be truthful, I wasn't lying about Noah and the whale. I just didn't know any better. I wasn't malicious. I was just incredibly stupid!

This brings me around to one of our recent presidents.

This past week I had an email from a friend, John Jorden, who wanted to run a few things by me. After reading his email, it dawned on me. Our esteemed former president isn't always lying to us. Sometimes, perhaps most of the time, he is just dumb. The man is just incredibly stupid.

Let me give you just one example:

You may remember a few weeks ago when being questioned about swapping prisoners at the end of the war, he said something to the effect that "three former Presidents made prisoner swaps **at the end of wars** that took place on their watch, "Much like this swap" he said.

The "this swap" he was referencing was his swap of five vicious terrorists out of Gitmo for Sgt. Bird-ball, or whatever the name of that deserter he got back, And then the president had the audacity to say,

"That is what happens at the end of wars. That was true of President George Washington, that was true of President Abraham Lincoln, and that was true President Franklin Roosevelt."

He continued, "That's been true of every combat situation. At some point, you make sure that you try to get your folks back. And that's the right thing to do." (CNN interview)

BEN GILL

That statement blatantly demonstrates that the most powerful man in the world and two-time President of the United States lacks even a grade school knowledge of American history.

When he was running for president the first time, you may remember him giving a speech and talking about the wonderful "57" states in our union. Folks, he wasn't lying to us by having knowledge of seven states that have been hidden from us. This man, who wanted to be and ultimately became our president, was just stupid. He thought there were 57 states.

Dear Lord, please help us all!

LIAR! LIAR! PANTS ON FIRE!!!!!

But back to this prisoner swap that he made because three other "great presidents did exactly the same thing." Let's just take a look at what history recorded.

Washington did not become president until six years after the Revolutionary War ended in 1783. By 1789 when he became president, there were no longer any prisoners for him to exchange.

Abraham Lincoln was assassinated in mid-April of 1865. The Civil War ended the following month. I looked it up! He was still dead at that time! No deals were made to exchange prisoners after the war. All prisoners were simply freed to go back home.

Finally, FDR died of a stroke before the end of WWII. Like Lincoln, **he stayed dead,** so after the war, he could not have done what our president said he did. You may recall that President Truman made the decision to use the atomic bombs on Japan, thus ending WWII. He made no deals for prisoners. We went in and released them when necessary.

None of the presidents referenced by the "57 states" president were in office at the end of those wars, making it impossible for them to make any prisoner swaps. So his swapping five radical Islamic terrorists plus an unspecified amount of cash for the deserter/traitor he got back was not based on a historical precedent. It really should be pointed out that countless deserters and traitors were executed during all the wars he referenced.

Frankly, I am not surprised that the president would get it wrong, but is there no one in his communications office, no one among his speech writers who checks facts for him?

Honestly, I now give him more credit than I have been giving him. This man is not dishonest. He is just incredibly dumb.

CHAPTER SEVENTEEN

Getting older requires much patience. I realized that recently when I had spent three days attempting to get a new prescription filled. Six calls, three visits to the pharmacy, and two days without the medication, and I still was in a holding pattern. Finally, today a fourth call brought the information we had been waiting to hear. My prescription would be $781 because "since the first of the year, your insurance no longer covers that medication."

It seems the prescription providers are following the same customer service set forth by the RingA-Ding phone service mentioned in an earlier chapter.

Patience, Gill! Patience!

Last night the news magazine "Sixth Minutes" reported on the rocketing costs of prescription drugs. Under the Obama Care Program, regulation of price was basically left up to the drug companies. So many drugs have gone up 1000-4000% in cost, making it almost impossible for the average person to afford non-insured care.

His Vice President liked the plan so much that he made the decision to renew it when he became president.

Patience, my boy! Patience!

We are fast becoming a nation of the "disconnected." More and more of our citizens are feeling disconnected from their nation, their long-term health organizations, their families, and, in some cases, from themselves.

Over a recent Thanksgiving Holiday, a group of people was standing around at the car dealership where each had brought their car in for service. This was at one of the most prestigious dealerships in San Fransisco. A place known for its personalized service.

This was before San Fransisco was taken over by thugs, and the city was destroyed. We will save that story for later.

But sometime since their last visit, the dealership had installed a new, totally automated service check-in process. Once you had called for an appointment, your date and time of service were scheduled. With that scheduling, you were then sent an email from the dealership confirming your appointment and asking if you would need a loaner car.

Arriving at the dealership at the appointed time, you were guided, by electronic signage no less, to the proper service lane. Another automated sign listed your name, auto information, and service needs. This information was taken from a chip embedded in your car at your previous service time.

At the end of that line, you find a display board with your information awaiting you. Without ever seeing a service person, you signed insurance forms, verified credit card information, were told when your car would be ready, and another sign directed you to the loan car area where your loaner awaited you with the key in the ignition and at least a half tank of gas.

You only had to drive away and return at the established time to pick up your now completely serviced vehicle. You had never interacted with any employee of the establishment.

That is what is meant by being disconnected!

Now for the rest of the story. I am told the

dealership had spent well over $2m on the system. It worked flawlessly. It did EXACTLY what it was designed to do. And after only six weeks, the dealership took its losses and killed the program. They rehired the service managers!

The message from the people was, "We do not want to be that disconnected."

Today I want to declare publicly that I do not want to be that disconnected either. I want to interact with people who laugh, cry, and like or hate me. I want to tell a joke and have someone laugh or groan. I want to cut my finger and have someone say, "Let me kiss that boo-boo for you."

Plug me in. I want to be a part of a world with people. People who will disagree with my opinions and will argue with me. People who will see my faults and help me correct them. I want to be around people where there is noise and chatter and song.

I may start a movement to get people to reconnect. This morning I went to the mall and just decided to speak to everyone I saw. No more head down dead heading to my destination. No, sir, today I would connect.

What a wonderful experience. Almost everyone spoke back, smiled, or gave a thumbs up. After 10 minutes in the mall, I felt better and sensed that some of those I had connected with felt better too.

Try it the next time you are out. There are absolutely no forms to fill out!

CHAPTER EIGHTEEN

THE CALL....He sat for a long time looking out the window of the cabin. Winter was coming to an end, and for perhaps the last morning of the season, there was frost on the ground. A slippery fog on the window gave his world a slightly out-of-focus image. Slightly out of focus was not only a pretty good description of the image but also a valid description of his life. Slightly out of focus...

Where had the years gone, and perhaps more importantly, why had they gone so fast?

She had died almost five years past. It was not an easy death, but as with most trials in their forty-five years together, they walked through it, giving and gaining strength from each other. When he lost his job and thought the world was over, she had given him hope. When she lost the second baby, he had given her a shoulder. In the jigsaw of life, it seemed all their pieces fit.

He remembered the day she told him. They called both kids, well, not kids anymore, each with a family of their own. "Mom has cancer," they shared while trying to hold all the emotions intact until the call could end. A few details, the expected "everything will be OK" and "we will keep you in touch as the treatments start." Tears flowed over wireless lines into heavy hearts, and then the call ended.

"Did we do the right thing in telling them?"

"I think so."

"Maybe this will be just a blip, and you will really respond to the treatment."

"I hope so," but she didn't "think" so.

The next few months were filled with all the "stuff" one does to attempt to prolong the inevitable. Her days passed with treatments doctors assured her would work. Nights were filled with haunting visions of what would happen if they didn't.

Most of all, she did not want to leave him. He was so utterly useless without her.

"Can you show me how this can opener works?"

"Where do we keep the toilet paper?"

"You mean we pay this guy this much just to keep the yard mowed?"

Useless.

Until he put his arm around her and held her while her system tried to purge all the poisons being injected to kill all the poisons already there.

Useless.

Until on their second Christmas after her diagnosis, he planned a weekend when the kids flew in with their families, and they had four wonderful days together.

Useless.

Until, in the fog of the last few days, they would spend together, she could look at him in his chair beside her bed and hear him whisper, "It's going to be OK."

But it wasn't OK. He had never known such loneliness. When she became sick, he quit his job to care for her, but now the days were far too long, and he had nothing to do except think.

Nights were longer, and sleep avoided him. Neighbors had finally stopped calling. There always comes a point when everything that could be said has been said, so another call just seems intrusive.

He had aged more in these five years since her passing than he cared to acknowledge. This man who had lived life on the edge was about to fall over that edge into nothingness.

So today, as the shadows fall and the world slips into night, he slips out of his chair and makes his way toward the kitchen. A few steps, and before he can fall, he steadies himself and sits on a chair at the kitchen table.

It is a prayer quietly said under his breath, "Oh God, if there is anything, any reason I need to keep on living, you need to tell me now."

Blasting into the silent room is the ringing phone. Quickly he moves toward the desk to answer on the third ring.

"Hi, Dad! The kids want to say Happy Father's Day."

CHAPTER NINETEEN

Holly and I have just returned today from four days in New York City. Boy, do I love that city! Over the years, we have gone many times, both on business and for pleasure, and each time I seem to see the city from a new perspective. On this trip, I decided to focus on the people I would meet. I wanted to get to know them as people and not just people who might fit my preconceived opinion.

No sooner had we landed and begun walking down the concourse at the airport than I saw a *New York Post* headline that confirmed the fact that we were indeed in New York. There in two-inch letters on the front page of the *Post*, were these words:

EXAMS AT COLUMBIA LAW
SCHOOL POSTPONED

STUDENTS TRAUMATIZED BY
RACE VERDICT

Yes! We have made it to the Big Apple! It seems the law students at Columbia University were so upset by the no-bill verdict brought by the Grand Jury in the choking death of one of the city's fine citizens that they simply could not take their exams.

Give me a BREAK! Keep in mind that these are the future attorneys who are going to be leading the cause for justice in the next very few years.

Can't you just hear them now.....

"Your Honor, I know I was to make closing arguments this morning, but last night, my dog got hit by a car, and I was so traumatized I am just not prepared. I can't give a closing argument today."

How in the world do these college graduates now in law school think the world works?

What if our soldiers operated like this? "Sorry, Captain, I saw a buddy killed yesterday, so I need to take a few days off to recover."

I would like to say "only in New York," but sadly, this is the American way these days.

Shoot, I am not even out of the airport, and I am already off track. I am here to focus on the real people of New York. Surely the Columbia law students are not a good example.

We got in a UBER Black Car for the trip into Manhattan. Our driver was a young man named Ban'da Har. Yep, right out of the Middle East. As we drove along, I noticed a cross hanging from his rearview mirror. I commented on the cross and then asked, "Ban'da, are you a Christian?"

"Oh yes," he replied. From that point on, our common denominator was our faith. He has been in the US for three years. He looked like a terrorist, he talked like a terrorist, and he was from the part of the world that breeds terrorists. But just like me, he was a Christian.

I wonder how many other people I have judged to be one thing when in reality, they are something else. The people of New York surprise me. And not just the people of NY, but the people who visit NY need also to be on my "getting to know you" list.

The next evening we were standing in line for a Broadway show when I overheard a conversation between two women in line behind us. Finally, as I am prone to do, I turned to them and said, "OK, I hear two very southern accents. Where are you fine ladies from?"

"Oh honey, we are from Arkansas!"

They were from Arkansas! They were from a small town about 100 miles from Dell, Arkansas, where I was raised. They had not heard of Uncle Red, but they had one brother and two cousins just like him. Finally, I introduced them to Holly and then asked them a question.

"We were talking last night about our wedding. Today is our wedding anniversary, and we were just wondering if we get a divorce, are we still first cousins."

Without blinking an eye, one replied, "Well, I sure hope so. If you ain't me and my brother, who have been married for 12 years, ain't got a chance."

Damn, I love Arkansas people!

The next day we saw a group of Salvation Army ladies dancing in the street with potential donors. I hope they raised a little money. They did bring much joy to the world. They were from the Bronx.

And that is the way the four-day visit went. Just talking to people. Laughing at one another. Getting to know more about our next Taxi driver, who was a Muslim and who let me know it even before I could ask.

I liked Brandon, the head waiter at a fine Italian restaurant. He was so overwhelmed by the press of the crowd wanting a table that when he took a young couple to their table, I stepped up to his desk and, for 10 minutes, did his job. I took names, hugged old ladies who were regulars at the restaurant, and just generally helped people have a good time.

At that point, we were still on a 90-minute wait-list, but when Brandon saw what I was doing, he gave me a big hug and whispered in my ear, "Get your party and follow me." With that, he directed us to a very nice table, hugged me again, and said, "God, I love you, man. Come in any time - I'll have a table for you."

Yes, sir, I do love New York. They are a special kind of people. They are gruff and rough on the outside but scrape down a little, and they are just like the rest of us.

Maybe it was just the Christmas Season that made everyone so warm and friendly.

Or maybe, just maybe, it was just New York!

CHAPTER TWENTY

I received an email this week from an elementary school student in Asia. The young man was fourteen years old. He shared that his English class used *Random Thoughts* each week as a study aid. Of all the many things I have written about over the past three years, the subject he was most interested in was dear old Uncle Red.

His question: "Will we ever get another Uncle Red story? We have come to enjoy him very much and would like to read another story about him."

What a wake-up call to this old blogger who, for almost three years, has written on many subjects. Religion, ethics, politics, emotions, depression, joy, and a myriad of other subjects have been sent into the Internet world, but the one most requested is just one more story about Uncle Red. Sort of says something about us, doesn't it?

Uncle Red was very influential in my life. It is interesting to realize now that he is touching another generation. So with no further discussion, allow me to share an event from my "Uncle Red Days" oh so long ago.

I was about twelve years old when I first learned the church service ended with a prayer. For the first twelve years of my life, I thought it ended with the whipping you got for being bad during the service. There is just so much to learn when you are just a kid.

But on this particular Sunday, the preacher had just said the opening prayer when the door of the sanctuary burst open. Suddenly making his way down the aisle was Uncle Red. There is no way to say this tactfully.

The old boy was soused. His face was redder than his hair, he was a little tipsy, and he was singing a quiet version of "You Ain't Nothing but a Hound Dog." The man had made an ENTRANCE.

There are three stained glass windows in that sanctuary with the name"Gill" emblazoned on them. One for my great-grandfather, one for my grandfather, and one for my father. When I saw Uncle Red enter the sanctuary, I swear all three windows shook.

He made his way to our pew and plopped down beside my Mom. Just as he sat down, the preacher said, "Today I will be preaching from John 3:16. Please open your Bibles."

The moment the preacher finished speaking, Red yelled out, "Amen, Brother! That is a fine verse you are using today, Rev! Preach on! Preach on!" All eyes were on Red, and Mom's hands were almost around his throat. If looks could kill, my Mom would have been a mass murderer.

Red then proceeded to sing a quiet verse of *Amazing Grace* while the preacher tried to maintain some dignity in the service. Red reached over and patted my head and said in a stage whisper, "Boy, listen to the preacher now. That man's got something to say to you. AMEN AND AMEN!"

This new liturgical pattern followed for the next 20 minutes. The preacher would say something, and Red would encourage him with a rousing "AMEN." Frankly, I was rather enjoying the show, but I could tell I was in the minority.

The kicker of the story comes when, at the end of the service, the preacher started to take up the morning offering. That was the last piece of the preaching puzzle needed to end the service.

Keep in mind that this one offering was the single funding method of the Dell Baptist Church. Whatever came in for the Sunday offering had to take care of all the expenses of the congregation for the next week, including the pastor's salary.

Well, the preacher made a nice pitch for the green. "Don't want to hear no loose change this morning. Folding money is more precious to the Lord." And just as he said that, Red stood up and raised his hand to the heavens.

"Preacher, just gimme the check. I got it covered today". Turning to the congregation, he said, "Put your money up, folks. I got the check today! This one is on me."

And with that, Red proceeded to have the closing prayer and send everyone on their way.

As a little kid, it was often possible to wander around in a crowd and eavesdrop on what was being said in small groups. I remember someone saying, "Red, thanks for covering things this week. I was a little short myself." About 20 other men all said, "Amen!"

A moment later, I heard the preacher asking Red

how he was going to take care of the charges. In his loud "look at me voice," Red proceeded to get his billfold out and said, "Well, Reverend, what's it take to run this place for a week?"

"Red, it takes about $300 week after week."

With that, Red reached into his pocket and pulled out a new $20 bill. "Reverend, this here is a start on it, and as you said last Sunday in your sermon, the Lord will provide - AMEN!"

I only heard one more comment before we left the church that day. It came from the preacher's office, and he was talking to his wife. "Get on your knees, woman. The offering was $210 short, and Red ain't good for it."

Then under his voice, I heard him say, "Damn those Gills! Damn, 'em to hell."

When I turned around, my Mom was standing behind me, and I realized she had heard every word. She looked at me and winked. She had a way of doing that as she took me by the hand. As we started for home, she looked down and said, "Well, your Uncle Red pulled a good one today, didn't he?"

She looked back over her shoulder at the people still leaving the church and, with a chuckle, said, "The old boy saved us some real money today." And with a skip in her walk, she continued, "Yep, the old boy saved us some money. Clap yo hands, son. Clap yo hands. And can you say AMEN, AMEN!"

CHAPTER TWENTY-ONE

Finally, summer was fading, and the cool nights of fall were just around the corner. Just two more weeks and I would be back in school where life would return to some familiar rhythm. A "familiar rhythm" is not all bad when you are fourteen years old and living in small town USA.

Uncle Red had called the night before and wanted me to be his golf partner at the opening of a new golf course in Jonesboro, AR. I had never swung a club, never been on a golf course, and never struck a ball. All of that was irrelevant to Uncle Red. He assured me he would teach me everything I needed to know. It seems we were to be playing with Mr. Perry Rose, the president of the First National Bank in Blytheville. A more prestigious financial institution could not be found in NE Arkansas.

Early the next morning, Red was sitting in front of my house, blasting away on the horn of his new Buick. When he saw me coming toward him, he got out of the car, and, folks, it was the craziest sight I have ever seen. Here stands Uncle Red with red knickers, a black shirt, and a funny-looking cap on his head. His bright orange shoes with nails in the bottom were the funniest part of the entire outfit.

Being the kind of stylist he was, the first thing he said was, "Don't let them shoes blow you away, son. We stopping at Sammy Cook's house and getting me some black ones before we play this afternoon."

Then he examined my attire:

"First, go get them jeans off. You can't wear no jeans on a nice course

like this, and whiles you up there, put on another shirt – one with some arms on it."

"What about shoes?" I asked.

"Well, we will have to do with what you got. Put on your tennis shoes and some white socks, and we will get by." A few minutes passed, and now knicker Red and white shoe Ben were ready to get down to my golf education. The lesson would fill most of the drive time to Jonesboro.

"Aw rite, boy, here is the things you needs to

know about golf. First, golf is a two-man team game. One of the team members hits the balls, and the other one carries the bag. Now today, you is going to be the one carrying the bag, so we don't need to teach you how to hit. Now, you got that so far?"

"Yeah, I got it." I could see right up front that until you got to be the hitter, this game was just going to be a lot of work.

He plowed on:

"It is your job to hand me a club when I need one. They is a mess of clubs in that bag, but I'll always tell you the one I want. You just have to remember that they is numbered from #2 up to #9. You see them that got them wool covers on them. They is called woods cause they is made out of a big block of wood, but you ain't ready for them yet.

"Now, when I want to hit the ball, I will tell you what number I want. On each hole, we get to start over at #2, so there is no need for you to do a lot of thinking. Here's how it works. I tell you to give me the four iron. I hit the ball with it. Now the next time I hit, I have to use the five iron. Then the six - you see how it works?"

"I think I'm getting the hang of it, but what about this one with a P on it and no number? Or what about this one that has 56 on it? What do I do with them?"

Man, I could tell he was getting frustrated with me, but he answered the question. According to Uncle Red, you used the "P" club when you wanted to punch it toward the hole. The "56" club was used when your score got to over 56 strokes. You could then use that club for a little added help. I don't know who thought up this game, but it sure had a lot of rules.

By this time, we had stopped at Sammy's house, and Uncle Red had new black golf shoes. I must say, when you put it all together, he was a dandy!

"Now, one last thing," he said with a great deal of seriousness in his voice. "They is libel to be a little skin in this game, so I want you to take your job seriously." He must have been serious because he did not say another word until we reached the Mudd Creek Country Club in Jonesboro. That twenty minutes of silence was a blessed reprieve from the game about to begin.

"You sit right here in the car, boy. I'm going in this here office place and let them know we is here. I'll be back in a minute."

In the past, every time Uncle Red told me to

wait in the car, I could expect at least an hour of just sitting there. But this time, things were different. He had not been in that office for five minutes when he comes storming back to the car, and his face was as red as the red in his knickers. I could tell he was powerfully upset.

"Boy, you got any money on you?"

"What do you think?"

"Well, them golf robbers in there want $10 for me to play the course. Now I got $3 myself. You sure you ain't got $7 more."

"I'm pretty dead sure, Red. So what are you going to do? You done told Mr. Rose you will play with him. You can't tell him you don't have any money. Jezz, you are in some kind of mess now."

About that time, Mr. Rose came out of the door and started over to our car. He is saying something about whether we need to hurry up, or we will miss our tee time or something like that. Panic was filling our car like rain filled the creek.

Quickly thinking through the situation, Uncle Red said to me, "Lie down on the floor and hold your stomach like you are really sick."

Before I can ask why Uncle Red has jumped out of the car and is shouting as loud as he can, "Lord,

Jesus, the boy is dying. I knew not to leave him in this hot car. Lordy, Lordy, Mr. Rose, call the hospital and tell them we are on our way. I'll have to play some other time. The blessed child is dying."

With that, he jumped in the car, threw her in first, and spun off toward the town. Last we saw Mr. Rose, was running to the golf office to make the call.

About a mile down the road Uncle Red pulled over to the side of the road and started laughing till tears fell down his face. Finally, when he could, he just reached over and rubbed my stubby red hair and said, "Well, Son. I guess there is one more lesson you need to learn about this game. If you ain't got no skin, then there ain't gonna be no game. What you say we go back to Mr. C.A.'s store and have us a big Orange."

CHAPTER TWENTY-TWO

I am going to introduce you to Dr. Ben Stein. Ben was an American writer, lawyer, actor, comedian, and commentator on political and economic issues.

He first came on the scene as a speechwriter for Richard Nixon and Gerald Ford but soon entered the field of entertainment as an actor, comedian, and game show host.

He was a funny, funny man and brought great joy to a generation of people who still knew how to laugh.

A few years ago, as our world started to fall into the numbness of disbelief about almost everything, I came across this article. I was so impressed that I made the decision to reprint and post it in my "Random Thoughts" blog.

I think there have been two times over the past

three years of writing this blog when I have turned this electronic pulpit over to someone else. Today is the third time. Ben Stein was a speechwriter for two US Presidents, has authored 16 books, acted in numerous movies, and is today a commentator on CBS Sunday Morning Commentary.

I have not met Ben, but from what I have heard of him, I think I would like him. He loves telling Jewish jokes, and he respects others' opinions. I think we would get along nicely.

It was surprising that CBS would allow him the freedom to present this commentary, but even more surprising that so many missed it. Allow me to turn this space over to Dr. Stein for a few words of wisdom:

The following was written by Ben Stein and recited by him on CBS Sunday Morning Commentary.

My confession:

I don't like getting pushed around for being a Jew, and I don't think Christians like getting pushed around for being Christians. I think people who believe in God are sick and tired of getting pushed around, period. I have no idea where the concept came from, that America is an explicitly atheist country. I can't find it in the Constitution, and I don't like it being shoved down my throat.

Or maybe I can put it another way: where did the idea come from that we should worship celebrities and we aren't allowed to worship God as we understand Him? I guess that's a sign that I'm getting old, too. But there are a lot of us who are wondering where these celebrities came from and where the America we knew went to.

In light of the many jokes we send to one another for a laugh, this is a little different: This is not intended to be a joke; it's not funny; it's intended to get you thinking. In light of recent events, terrorist attacks, school shootings, etc. I think it started when Madeleine Murray O'Hare (she was murdered, and her body was found a few years ago) complained that she didn't want prayer in our schools, and we said OK. Then someone said you better not read the Bible in school. The Bible says thou shalt not kill; thou shalt not steal, and love your neighbor as yourself. And we said OK.

Then Dr. Benjamin Spock said we shouldn't spank our children when they misbehave because their little personalities would be warped and we might damage their self-esteem (Dr. Spock's son committed suicide). We said an expert should know what he's talking about. And we said okay.

Now we're asking ourselves why our children have no conscience, why they don't know right from wrong, and why it doesn't bother them to kill strangers, their classmates, and themselves.

Probably, if we think about it long and hard enough, we can figure it out. I think it has a great deal to do with, 'WE REAP WHAT WE SOW."

Funny how simple it is for people to trash God and then wonder why the world's going to hell. Funny how we believe what the newspapers say but question what the Bible says. It's funny how you can send 'jokes' through e-mail, and they spread like wildfire, but when you start sending messages regarding the Lord, people think twice about sharing. Funny how lewd, crude, vulgar, and obscene articles pass freely through cyberspace, but public discussion of God is suppressed in the school and the workplace.

Are you laughing yet?

Funny how when you forward this message, you will not send it to many on your address list because you're not sure what they believe or what they will think of you for sending it.

Funny how we can be more worried about what other people think of us than what God thinks of us.

Pass it on if you think it has merit.

If not, then just discard it. No one will know you did. But, if you discard this thought process, don't sit back and complain about what bad shape the world is in.

My Best Regards, Honestly and Respectfully,

Ben Stein

CHAPTER TWENTY-THREE

I have been told by people in the "blog for public consumption" business that it is important not to write about your own family. Seems that is unprofessional, and usually, the content is not very interesting. Obviously, those blog experts have never met my family.

Frankly, (IPCT) I thought it was pretty funny when Uncle Renfro burned his house down while trying to kill an ant infestation. I suppose it was serious at the time, but there is something about spraying gasoline in the kitchen cabinet and then throwing a match in to kill the ants that just strikes me as funny. Sure, Aunt Rose almost died before she could get dressed and out of the house before the roof fell in, but other than that, I thought it was a hoot.

Shot, I even chuckle thinking about my cousin

Harmon shooting his brother's ear off at the 1956 family summer reunion at the park in Blytheville, Arkansas. Granted, it was on a dare, and granted, there was some Jim Beam in the area, but the event itself was hilarious. Seems someone in the family had read about this historical guy who shot an apple off the head of someone. Of course, he used an arrow or something other than the 22 pistol Harmon had in his pickup.

I was pretty young, but I can still vividly remember little Bobby standing up against a tree while Harmon carefully placed the apple on his head. Someone probably should have stopped Harmon after seeing him drop the apple three times just trying to get it to sit on Bobby's head. But what can I say? No one did.

By this time, all the men and a few of the women in the family have gathered around to watch the historical reenactment. A few people have wandered over from other family groups in the park. There is a lot of murmuring in the crowd, and a few bets are being placed. The amazing thing is that the bets are on whether or not Harmon will hit or miss the apple. It never dawned on people that the great bet of the day might be whether or not little Bobby would live to old age. But I digress.

Finally, everything is in place. Bobby is against the tree with an apple on his head, and Harmon has stepped off 25 feet and has aimed the 22 pistol directly at Bobby. Just as he gets set, a wasp lands on his arm, and in a moment of self-preservation, Harmon swats at the wasp and simultaneously fires the gun. (IPCT) That moment remains one of the most memorable in our summer reunion stories, and to this day, Bobby has a hole the size of a dime through his left ear.

Now I don't care who you are. I think that is funny whether it happened in my family or not. Give me a man who doesn't think that is funny, and I'll show you a man who has lace on his panties. Show me a woman who doesn't have to stifle a smile while she is proclaiming how dumb men are, and I'll show you a woman with no sense of humor.

Well, now that wasn't even what I started to write about. My initial intention was to write about the economy and how we as a nation have grown accustomed to spending for what we want and not necessarily for what we need. I was debating whether or not, to begin with a family story to illustrate the point when I was confronted by the "no personal story" rule.

So just pretend the next sentence is the first sentence of this week's blog.

He was sixteen, a high school senior, and the prom was only a few weeks away. My son was getting ready for the big event and wanted it to be special. He had ordered his tux and was making arrangements for the pre-prom dinner. Wanting to take his date to a very special place, he approached me and asked if he could use my membership to take her to the University Club. I agreed on the condition that he pay for the dinner. He agreed, and reservations were made.

The University Club in Dallas during that time was sheer opulence. And it was very expensive. So trying to save the boy from financial ruin, I coached him on the ordering process. I explained that he would receive a menu with the prices on it but that his date's menu would not have prices printed. Therefore, it would be to his financial benefit to guide her through the process. I explained that the chicken cordon bleu was the least expensive thing on the menu, so he should say something like this:

"You know my dad eats here a lot, and he tells me the chicken cordon bleu is delicious. Would you like to try that this evening?"

Then with my years of experience guiding me, I explained to him that she would order the chicken, he would get out at the lowest possible price, and it would be a successful evening.

The pictures are all taken, and the kids are off for their big night at the prom.

About midnight there is a loud, urgent knock on my bedroom door. Afraid that something terrible has happened, I rush to the door, only to find my son seated on the floor. I fall to the floor beside him,

"What's the matter?" I ask in a panic, "Has something happened. What's the matter?"

"Dad, oh, Dad! She ordered lobster. Dad, what does market price mean?"

And in that personal story from our family history, you have America in a nutshell. As a nation, we were guided by history and brilliant leaders to order chicken, and what did we do? We spent the last twenty or thirty years feasting on lobster.

Now the payment is coming due. The price is more than we expected. But unfortunately, we have to live with our choice. Whether or not you have been politically active in the past is irrelevant. Now you and I have no choice. If we want to save this country, we had better get involved and start electing officials who understand there is a day when we must pay for the lobster.

And starting right now, we had all better get used to chicken or, perhaps, the vegetable plate.

Write it down!

CHAPTER TWENTY-FOUR

If you are in a relationship that is broken today, this chapter was written especially for you. Perhaps you are a parent with a strained relationship between you and your child. Maybe a sister is not speaking to a sibling. Perhaps you have had a falling out with a neighbor, or maybe a distant relative has disappointed you. You get the drift; people, because we are people, sometimes disagree, and very often, those disagreements lead to strained or broken relationships.

If you are like me, those periods in a relationship are always troubling. I am uneasy and stressed when all the pieces are not falling into their proper place. I remember once when I was in college. I did something that caused a crack in the relationship I had with my mother. I worried about that disruption for days until, at last, one of us called; I don't remember who reached out first to say, "I don't like this feeling between us. Let's bury the hatchet and forget about what has happened."

That day was a day filled with joy. A broken circle of love had been mended. It is that type of experience that leads us to this blog today. Please read on with an open heart. This could be a day to remember in your life.

Today we are going to think about the concept of "forgiveness" and how forgiveness fits into our lives in today's world. This subject has been on my mind for several weeks, and with a detective's curiosity, I have listened to and watched others deal with this subject. I have looked for clues as to why forgiveness is needed and why, in many cases, it is never found.

I have probed into the crevices of the mind to examine why some people can easily forgive while others seem to hold on to the events requiring forgiveness as they might hold on to their most precious possessions.

At this moment, I do not know whether I will look at forgiveness from a Biblical perspective or not. Right now - at the beginning of this intellectual pilgrimage, I am more interested in the impact forgiveness has on us at the moment than I am in its eternal effects. Let me share a couple of examples from real life:

Little Johnny hits little Bobby, and within seconds little Bobby has

1. stopped crying,
2. hugged little Johnny, and
3. resumed playing.

But little Bobby's mother picks up little Bobby and

1. takes him home,
2. tells all the neighbors what little Johnny did,
3. becomes so consumed with the event that she cannot sleep, and
4. finally files suit against little Johnny's family claiming "lifetime damages to her family."

The case has been in court for four years, and finally, now big Johnny is made a ward of the court and assigned to juvenile detention. Then the judge rules in favor of the plaintiff for $10 million. Johnny's parents finally get a divorce caused by the stress of the past four years. When big Bobby is asked about the case, he tells the reporter, "I didn't remember the incident. I guess I was just too young."

And the event that triggered these events probably took no more than five minutes on a children's playground.

Sadly it took very little creativity to develop that scenario.

A few years ago, I was talking with a friend from St. Louis as we flew to Seattle together. His family had been visiting him in Colorado each summer for several years. It seemed the entire family had a wonderful time in the mountains. They fished, hiked, sat by a campfire, and did all the things associated with this wonderful place.

As he talked about the time with his family, he seemed to glow with pride and joy. The event would be long remembered in the lore of the family, and as his three children left to go home, the stories of the week would be carried across the land as they shared this family event with others.

After a break of a couple of years, his family came back this year. After their visit was over and they had returned to their homes, I talked to him again and found the joy of the previous trip had not been experienced on this visit. Finally, he said, "Sue

Ann didn't come to the reunion this year." Sue Ann is his 32-year-old single daughter, the youngest of his children.

"Last Christmas, I said something that offended her. I don't remember much about what I said. You know, just something was offensive to her beliefs, memories, or something. She didn't say anything at the time. She just let her mother know that she was offended by me and never wanted to have contact with me again. I tried to reach out to her, but she wasn't interested. I've apologized. I've tried leaving her alone. I don't know what she wants. Just one little statement and I lost her. It just wasn't the same this year."

I don't know what happened in that family. But as far as I know, everything was wonderful with the relationship each person had with the other. And in one sentence, maybe one discussion but, at most, one tiny event at Christmas, everything good was set aside in order for a daughter to show (shot I can't think of a word) resentment (maybe) to her father. And now they don't speak or keep in contact. And as happens so often in these cases, no one won.

Let's pull the example of Sue Ann apart and look at it. If Sue Ann is 32 years old, she has known her father for 16,819,200 minutes in her lifetime. Let's assume her father's discussion with her that Christmas lasted one hour. Probably just a few brief minutes if the truth were known. But Sue Ann is willing to set aside the other 16,819,140 wonderful minutes of their relationship because of one hour in which she felt offended.

Sixty minutes out of 16,819,200 minutes. Sounds sort of insignificant, doesn't it?

Does that sound logical or reasonable to you? It doesn't to me. I kept asking myself what had been building all through the years that would cause this relationship to culminate in one hour of disagreement.

We probably will never know, but isn't it a shame that one hour could have that much impact on a lifetime?

When I step back and consider the experiences of Johnny and Sue Ann, I wonder if a bit of "forgiveness" could have brought joy and hilarity to them and their families. In each case, the people involved brought pain and sadness when a tiny bit of forgiveness could have changed the entire ending.

Perhaps forgiveness should be looked at from a theological viewpoint. Jesus provided such a perfect example for us. God's Son comes to us and walks among us. We accuse, reject and ultimately kill him. interestingly enough, he lived 32 years also (Sue Ann, check the parallel here).

And how does he use it when given His last moment out of his 16,819,200 minutes? He speaks a phrase that has eternal implications: "Father, forgive them, for they know not what they do." And then He died. Because He chose to use His hour to forgive and not to hate or reject life for each of us; life is better.

It is amazing what a little bit of forgiveness can do for us and for others whose lives we touch. Don't blow 16,819,200 minutes of life just because something unpleasant happened in a brief few of them. A statement made, a feeling felt, or an emotion experienced in a single moment is not worth destroying a lifetime relationship.

Think about it.

So how can this change your life? The process is very simple. If you are in a broken or strained relationship, why don't you consider contacting that person today? A phone call would be the best way, but I do understand that we live in an "email" world. The important thing is to make contact. Say something like this:

"I just wanted to say to you that I am sorry our relationship has been strained these last few (months, years, etc.). I want you to know that I miss you and want to have your friendship back in my life. Where I have failed and been wrong, I am sorry. I am asking you to accept me back in your life again."

Of course, you will change this to fit your situation, but you get the drift. Don't rehash the problem, and don't lay blame. Your message is very simple. I want us to reconnect, and I am willing to take the first step to see that happen.

If you get a chance after you have taken this step, drop me an email (txben@me.com) and let me know what happens. I think you will find it one of the most valuable moments in your life.

CHAPTER TWENTY-FIVE

I sit here on April 13, 2023, and listen to the news of a twenty-one-year-old US National Guard member who has unloaded this nation's most secret information to our friends and enemies.

More troubling than the fact that the information was leaked is the fact that a twenty-one-year-old kid had access to our most sensitive secrets.

Secrets of the arms build-up in China were in the documents. Secrets of the Urkranin battle plans against Russia were found floating around after the leaked documents were reviewed. The US knowledge of Egypt's plan to sell arms to Russia was detailed. Oh, yes, don't forget those arms were sold to Egypt by the US, probably at a far lower price than Egypt will receive from Russia.

Traveling on a goodwill tour to Ireland, our president, Mr. Biden, said when asked about the security leak:

"Oh, it's no big deal."

Months ago, when asked about the runaway inflation the US is facing, the President said,

"Oh, it's no big deal."

Previously, when gas prices were hovering around $5.00 a gallon nationally, he assured the American people of America could absorb the high cost. Here it is again, "Oh, it's no big deal."

Sometime after assuring the American people that gas prices were not a problem, eggs were selling for $7.00 a dozen.

"Oh, it's no big deal."

What about that pullout from Afghanistan? We walked off, leaving $83 BILLION of planes, trains, jeeps, tents, rifles, and automobiles, plus a few billion in ammunition, socks, and junk like that. Then we left a few thousand Afgan troops, who were fighting for us, behind so the Taliban could kill them. Then we had some of our largest transport planes take off with our friends hanging from the wheels as the planes flew toward altitude. What did Biden have to say?

"It was a well-thought-out departure. There were a few glitches, but all in all, It's no big deal."

Rather than going on and on, let's just get to the point. It is one thing when the American people are taken by surprise, but when they are warned and then still screw up, it is their own fault. In this case, it was crystal clear.

We were actually warned by the man who chose Biden as the VP nominee for two terms.

At the end of those two terms, President Obama had just one message to the American people:

"Don't ever underestimate Joe's ability to f...k things up."

And old Uncle Joe said, "Oh, it's no big deal," as he went on the win the election.

CHAPTER TWENTY-SIX

Memory has never been my strongest attribute. For most of my adult life, I have suffered, yes, suffered from the affliction of memory loss. For instance, with no disrespect to anyone, I have always been able to meet you, look you in the eye, and repeat your name when you were introduced to me, only to forget your name within 30 seconds. This has caused me much humiliation in days past.

I remember one time we had a guest speaker coming to our office to speak to our staff. This man was a known national celebrity who was mobbed at the airport as he came into Dallas. His first engagement was to speak at our staff luncheon. Including a few invited guests, he would be speaking to about 250 people.

Just to be certain I introduced him properly, I

wrote extensive notes on his background. I memorized those notes for days in preparation for this event. At the appointed time, I went to the podium to introduce our famous guest. As I looked at the notes I had prepared, it dawned on me that I had not written down his name. And standing there with the world watching, I did not have a clue who he was. Oh, I knew he was the CEO of a Fortune 500 company, I just could not for the life of me think of his name.

The introduction went something like this:

"We are so honored to have my good friend here to speak to us today (no mention of his name). This fine man is the CEO of one of the most respected companies in America (still no mention of the name).

As the founder of his own company, there is much we can learn from him"

I continued to flounder while most of my staff, who were all well aware that once again I had failed the memory test, tried to keep from laughing.

Finally, in desperation, I closed the introduction by saying, "As he comes to speak to us today, one of the first things I want him to do is pronounce his name for us. As an old country boy from Arkansas,

I have a hard time with fancy names. So come now and share with us." See how I used humor to save my butt.

With a bemused look on his face, our guest came to the podium, shook hands with me, and leaned into the mike, "Yea, Ben, it's a hard one. Ladies and gentlemen, I am Fred Smith, and I bring you greetings from your friends at Fed Ex."

Multiply that a thousand times, and you have my lifetime war with memory.

About four years ago, I was playing golf with my regular foursome plus another guest at the Country Club of the Rockies in Colorado. All four of my playing partners were close friends. It was a normal day, not excessively hot. A slight breeze was blowing, and all was right with the world. As the fifth player, I was in a cart by myself, just enjoying the day.

We had completed the first four holes and were now standing on the fifth tee box. This hole is a straight, par four with sand traps on each side of the fairway. We all teed off, and as our three carts made our way down the fairway, it dawned on me that I did not know whether or not I was in Colorado or back at my club in Dallas.

Everyone made the second shot, and the other carts pulled ahead, racing to the green. I held back a bit and looked around at the setting.

There were mountains on my left. This must be Colorado. But when I got to the green, there were four people there, and I did not know any of them. One man was standing waiting to putt, and when I got his attention, I called him over.

"Look, who are these people? I know I am supposed to know, but I don't know who you are."

"Ben, I am K.O. Dixon, and we play golf together every week."

I knew none of them. I was suffering from dehydration, and my mind had stopped functioning. Very quickly, they called 911, and an ambulance came and took me to the hospital, and after three IV bottles of fluids, things began to come back into focus for me. It was a frightening experience.

Now here is the strange part of the story. About a week later, I took my car to have the oil changed. As I started to leave it, the mechanic said to me, "Why are you changing the oil again? It says here that we changed it ten days ago." It had been totally blocked out of my mind.

Over the next few days, by checking my calendar and having Holly quiz me on things we had done, I realized I had lost the memory of twenty days. It was as though they had never happened. Fifteen years later and I still cannot remember one thing from those twenty days.

Segue. That is exactly what God does when we confess our sins to Him and accept His forgiveness through Christ. I look back at my life before becoming a Christian, and sometimes I agonize over the stupid, sinful things I did.

And sometimes, in prayer, I start to confess them all over again, and every time it is as though God says, "What are you talking about? I have no memory of your life before you came to me. Forget it! It's over and forgotten."

What an incredible gift He offers us! How wonderful to have God say to us, "I have no idea what you are talking about."

CHAPTER TWENTY-SEVEN

Today the Middle East is on fire, and unless something dramatic is done, that area of the world will fall to radical Islamists. Many feel this is one of the first steps toward world domination by these radical fanatics. Stay tuned. We have many months and, hopefully, years to watch this unfold.

But as Americans, we are in another war. This war is less visible, gets almost no press, and is a reflection of what is taking place around the world.

This is the war against the Christian faith, and it is a war that is escalating in America. The focus of this war seems to be the educational system. It is a war directed toward our children through a system whose educational focus seems to be diverted from educating our children to blatant indoctrination.

Everyday stories to back this up come across my desk. Let me give you a sample:

School Officials Redacts God from Speech

The young man's name is Brooks Hamby, a high school salutatorian whose graduation speech was censored by school officials three times.

This was a national news story ONLY on Fox News on June 16.

Brooks is a quiet young man, a good student, obviously, and a Christian. When he was called to confirm his status as salutatorian, he was told he would be giving a speech at the graduation ceremonies. As part of the process, he was to submit his speech to school officials for approval.

The first submission was turned down because he had written it as a prayer, including the sentence: "Heavenly Father, in all times, let us always be kind to one another, tenderhearted, forgiving one another, as God in Christ has forgiven us." The school officials promptly rejected his text. He then submitted a second draft that mentioned the censorship of the first draft. The school district also objected to the second version of his speech.

In a warning letter from school officials, Brooks was told that:

> "*The first and second draft speeches proposed oppose government case law and are a violation of the Constitution. The District is advising you that reference to religious content is inappropriate and that the two drafts provided will not be allowed.*"

As would be found in the Ninth Circuit, this was a lie.

On graduation day, Brooks referenced his three drafts of his speech and then made this amazing statement:

> "*No man or woman has ever truly succeeded or been fulfilled on the account of living for others and not standing on what they knew in their heart was right and good.*"

The school board had made an outrageous attempt to silence religious speech. Without the counsel of First Liberty[17], an organization in Plano, TX, seeking to uphold free religious rights in America, they might have won. Instead, even the Ninth Circuit (the most liberal in America) wrote that **no government official may censor simple references to God.**

What had been an attempt to silence, in this case, a Christian voice, was defeated by the Constitution.

Obama Announces Plans For A Third-Term Presidential Run

Senator Rand Paul of Kentucky told CNN he does not agree with Obama and his announcement. "This defies everything the Constitution stands for," Paul said. "We cannot let this man have a third term."

In the history of this country, only two presidents have served more than two terms, Theodore Roosevelt and Franklin D. Roosevelt. The major problem for Obama when he runs in 2016 is the 22nd Amendment. In short, the 22nd Amendment states, "No person shall be elected to the office of the President more than twice..."

The U.S. Constitution does make an exception in the 22nd Amendment though: "This article shall be inoperative unless it shall have been ratified as an amendment to the Constitution by the legislatures of three-fourths of the several states within seven years from the date of its submission to the states by the

Congress." This means Obama's third-term presidential run is only valid if he receives 75% approval from Congress.

A bill to abolish the 22nd Amendment was recently introduced into Congress by New York Democratic Rep. Jose Serrano and is gaining popularity. This is exactly the kind of news that makes an Obama 2016 Presidential run possible.

Paul Horner, who is a spokesman for the Obama Administration, told reporters how amazing this news is for the country. "Obama is guaranteed to win in 2016, and then we'll all be able to enjoy this great man for another four years. Things could not get any better for the American people. I'm so stoked!"

When Angela Hildenbrand, a model high school student, and valedictorian, was threatened with jail by a federal judge if she prayed during her graduation speech, many were shocked. The judge issued a restraining order against her and said anyone mentioning God during her graduation ceremony would be sent to jail.

Again First Liberty was called, and they immediately filed an emergency motion for intervention and sought relief from the temporary restraining order. The U.S. Court of Appeals for the Fifth Circuit overturned the ruling. But in this case, a school board and a federal judge had joined efforts to kill Angela's religious rights. Because someone stood up to them, they were beaten in court, and Angela was allowed to exercise her constitutional right to freely express her religious rights.

Case after case of similar situations are coming before the courts. In 2018 some 1200 cases were fought for the religious rights of grade school, high school, and university students. Even if the cases were won, the magnitude of attacks and attacks blatantly attempting to shut down individual religious rights continue to grow.

If you are a Christian, you are at war with those who would quiet our faith.

The war is growing even faster in the military. A student at the Air Force Academy was threatened by expulsion if he did not remove a

scripture verse written on a whiteboard in his OWN private dorm room.

In another case, another officer gave Sgt. Phillip Monk an order to renounce his faith. If he did not agree with the atheist officer, he was told he would be given a dishonorable discharge. Sgt. Monk was a combat veteran with 19 years of service. If he was dishonorably discharged, he would lose all his pension and other benefits.

Again First Liberty was called in, and not only was the officer reprimanded, but orders were issued from the Pentagon that students could exercise their religious rights.

But what if no one had stood up for Phillip Monk? What, then, would have happened?

These cases are becoming so frequent in military circles that First Liberty has recently opened another division whose responsibility is to defend military personnel from such attacks.

And it is not just in America that the battles of this war are being fought.

Recently, ISIS wiped out an entire Christian city in Iraq because they were not Muslims. A city that had stood for almost 1700 years was destroyed simply because most of the citizens were Christian.

In Egypt, the COPTS are being destroyed because they believe in Jesus. Hundreds of years of peaceful co-existence have been put aside because the Muslim Brotherhood was offended by their Christian faith.

Across Africa, Christians die for their faith. North Korea imprisons tourists who speak of God in their ungodly country.

Other Anti-Christian events on the list include:

NBC television network twice took out the words "under God" from the Pledge of Allegiance in its lead-up to the U.S. Open at the Congressional Country Club.

In Franklin, Mass., a pro-life man was beaten by the police for peacefully handing out pro-life materials. The police accused him of conspiring to plant bombs.

A Christian man in Minnesota was fired from his job because one of his female co-workers attended a Bible Study that his wife led.

A Florida Christian teacher was suspended after school administrators discovered his support of traditional marriage posted on the Internet.

In Kalispell, Mont., pro-lifers were attacked by a firebomb during a prayer vigil in front of an abortion clinic. No one was hurt, but a police officer remarked that pro-lifers should expect this sort of reaction to their activities.

Because of a complaint filed by the ACLU, the liberal 9th Circuit Court ruled that the Mt. Soledad

War Memorial in San Diego was unconstitutional. Fortunately, that decision was later overturned by the Supreme Court.

A homosexual activist effort prompted investigations by the online money-transfer company PayPal against pro-family Christian organizations.

A Bible study was shut down by San Juan Capistrano, Calif., officials who claimed the group needed a permit because it posed a risk to public safety and health.

On and on, I could go, but the message is that we are at war. We need to start reinforcing our faith because the days may be few before we, too, are asked to stand for our faith. Whether you are a Christian, Jew, Muslim, atheist, or agnostic, we all have a dog in this fight. As someone once wrote, "If they can kill the Jew today, just know they can kill you tomorrow."

CHAPTER TWENTY-EIGHT

On Monday, two weeks before the 2014 Master's Tournament, the call that every golfer dreams of receiving came to my cell. "Ben, I have an opportunity to play Augusta on Tuesday, and I can bring a guest. How about being my partner?"

I have been to Augusta for the Masters. I walked the course early in the morning, just before the tees were set for the championship round. But in my wildest dreams, I have never teed up on the first tee and played where the big boys play. An excited "yes," a quick pack of the bags to get to the airport, and two hours later, I was seated in a Netjet Challenger on my way to the greatest day of golf I have ever experienced.

Let me warn you, this is going to be a long blog. If you are a golfer, you will understand. If you are not, then please just read what you can and wait for something better next week. This was my day, and I am going to relive every moment.

The course was set up for the 2006 Masters, still seven days away, so the number one tee was set for 445 yards. Since our foursome were all rank amateurs, temporary tees were set up, making the number one flag on the Tea Olive hole just a 397-yard, par four. Those 397 yards looked like a mile as we stood on that first tee.

Since members prefer to remain anonymous, I will just call them by their first names. It is a tradition at Augusta. In fact, everything is a tradition at Augusta. As the ranking member at Augusta, our host, Jack, stepped to the tee and drove his shot straight down the center.

A good 275 yards from the tee, leaving a short second shot to the green.

Bob and Charles made their drive look easy; now, it was up to me. I will have to admit I thought no golf shot could be harder than the #1 tee shot at Pebble Beach with 40-50 spectators standing nose to nose with you, but believe me; nothing is as nerve-wracking as hitting that first ball at Augusta. Only the four of us were there. No noise, no spectators, just my playing partners and me, and yet my legs were like jelly.

I am old, and I am short, but I can usually hit a driver. With determination, I hit that drive with everything I had and watched it settle down the fairway. I was short of the others but by just a little. And I was in play. I considered that a victory.

My ball was out, so the second shot honors were mine. I misjudged the wind, and my nine-iron did not get me to the green, but I was only 7 yards out. A soft wedge should put me on the green about a foot from the hole. Bill and Charles placed their second shots on the green. Bob hit the front left bunker and buried one in the sand.

Finally, with each of us putting for par, the game was on. All four balls dropped for pars. Let me die and go to heaven. I have made a par on a hole at Augusta - just like the big boys do.

The day moved on, and before we knew it, we were at #12 in the heart of Amen Corner.

At this spot in 1999, Holly and I sat behind the tee box and heard Tiger's caddie say to him, "Twelve inches right of the stick and twenty-four inches forward, there is a soft spot. If you hit there, your ball will stick but won't roll. So stay away from that spot."

Now I stood on that same tee box and just prayed to hit the green. At 155 yards, this is the shortest hole on the course, but it can be a game-killer. A little left and you end up off the green in the back. A little right, and you can catch the edge and roll back into the creek. With those caddie words from five years back sounding in my ears,

I stepped to the tee. I just needed a solid seven iron......

The ball hit the green about two yards past the hole, and then it did something my ball never does. It spun backward and slowly rolled to within three inches of the hole. The gallery made up only of whispering pines shouted to the heavens. I would go on and win the hole after making my three-inch birdie putt.

All around the course, there were memories. That is where Tiger chipped in from about 30 feet out. Here is where Bubba hit that long slow hook to save his round. Hogan always liked this hole. Jack plugged this bunker and took a three to get out.

Before I knew it, we were on #18. Standing on the tee box, both Bob and I were tied for the lead. Thank goodness for the handicap system that keeps an average player like me in the game. Good tee shots through that alley of trees put us up by the left bunker with a clear view of the green. The green is guarded by two bunkers, the fairway is all uphill, and just behind the green sits that awesome clubhouse.

Waiting to hit my second shot, I thought of all the leaders who had walked up this fairway on Master's Sunday. And now it was my time.

I was still 175 yards out, so I took my #5 fairway wood and gave it all I had left in me. The ball rose up the hill like a glider in flight, and we all watched as it glided onto that final green and rolled into the back corner. I was a good 45' from the hole with Bob about to make his second shot.

His shot was a work of art. It sailed in the breeze until finally landing on the green and rolling just one foot behind mine. He would have the first putt, and I could watch the line. Our partners were both short of the green on their second shot. With the grace of true sportsmen everywhere, they played on out and left Bob and me to putt for the win.

Since my ball was in his line, I marked it and stepped aside. Jack Nicklaus said that his greatest accomplishment was never wishing an opponent a missed shot. Well, I learned that day that I am no Jack Nicklaus.

Bob lined up his putt and went for the pin. His ball seemed straight dead on until about six feet out when slowly, very slowly, his ball slid right and ran by the pin. He had missed the hole by less than an inch, and his ball came to rest about eight inches from the pin. It sat there waiting for his last shot for par. If I was to win, it would take a miracle 50-foot putt along the same line.

I play a Niki ball, and as I placed my ball on the green, I knew in my heart I could make the putt for a birdie and the match. I had waited too many years to make this putt. I simply could not miss it.

Stroking the ball, I knew the moment it left my putter, it was on the line. Everything was in slow motion. When the ball came to the breakpoint where Bob's ball had taken a dive right, my ball was just high enough to hold the line.

I held my breath as it rolled toward the hole.

I felt the shaking immediately. My entire body was being tossed about. And what was that noise? Listen - what is that I hear?

"Ben, Ben, wake up. You have that meeting downtown, and your clock didn't go off. Get up. You are going to be late. Ben! I laid out your suit, and the coffee is about ready. Get up now!

Oh no! It was a dream. Just a dream! I still don't know if I made the putt.

CHAPTER TWENTY-NINE

I am writing this on Tuesday, November 11. This is Veteran's Day in the US, and it is an important time for remembering. On this day, we honor those who fought for our freedom and for the freedom of others. There are not many days as important to the heart of a true patriot as this one. While some don't, those of us who know and remember the horrors of war stand a little taller when we watch our veterans pass by.

Over the past few years, I have told you many things about Uncle Red, but the most important thing you might want to know about him is that he was a veteran. As a very young man, he went off to Korea to stem the spread of communism. He once told me he had been captured by the North Koreans and held captive for four days. His story was that after hearing redneck stories for four days, the enemy let him go.

Somehow I don't believe that, but after everything else he did, maybe it was true.

I have written about my Uncle Bill, who signed up at 16 to fight in WWII. He was a tail gunner in one of those big bombers, a B-17 Flying Fortress that hit Germany so hard. We got the telegram telling us he was missing in action on a cold December night. I remember standing around a pot belly stove with other members of the family as we read that message. Many a tear fell that night for a kid who died for his country.

Like every family, we had some who made it home from the wars and a few who didn't. Gill and Gilmer (my mother's maiden name) spilled blood on the mountains of Korea. But we spilled our blood not only there but in Germany, Vietnam, and a few other spots around the world. Our family is just like yours. We have fought for America.

It bothers me to see some people wanting to disrespect this country after so many have given so much to help us survive. I watched the news over the weekend as the prisoners who had been held in North Korea got off the plane to stand on American soil once again.

One of those returning was a very young man

who had gone to North Korea and then torn up his US citizenship papers. He said he wanted to denounce his American citizenship and live in that wonderful land ruled by Kim Jun IL Dig Dong or whatever his name is. Frankly, as far as I am concerned, they could have kept him.

For everyone like that, thousands have died in order for him to have a land willing to welcome him back.

Last night it was warm in Dallas. This was prior to our permanent move to Colorado. As was often the case, Holly and I walked through our neighborhood, and it was a nice time just to talk and be together. The high for today is supposed to be 40 degrees as the polar vortex blows in and turns things to winter.

At 10:00 this morning, the wind is expected to gust to 40-50 mph, with a wind chill around 20 degrees. But long before the weather changed, a group of our citizens planned the annual Veteran's Day Parade that is scheduled to begin in about four hours.

So the Gill family will be bundling up with gloves and hats. We will walk downtown for the parade. We will not go for the bands or even the marching horses with the soldiers on their backs.

The floats are nice, but that is not why we will go. No, we will go because someone's son or daughter, mother or father, brother or sister will be honored for their service to our country.

Around here, we believe that if they can stand on the front lines to protect us, we can stand on the curb and show our appreciation. Here we salute those who have served. Hold your head high and accept our appreciation. Thank you for "standing tall" for America.

God bless you, and God bless the United States of America.

CHAPTER THIRTY

I did not know Robin Williams, but I knew his killer. I have written about this killer several times since beginning this blog. I always warned you about it. I called it the "Dark Side." I portrayed it as a "black hole" in the middle of life. But I did not joke about

it because, far too many times, this killer stalked me, frightened me in the middle of the night, and destroyed my peaceful existence.

Last year Holly and I went to the Vilar Center here in Beaver Creek, Colorado, to

see Robin Williams in his One Man Show. He was profane, loud, spontaneous, irreverent, and funny. Most of all funny. But as we drove home, we both commented on the sadness on his face. We attributed it to fatigue or altitude. Both usually impact visitors to this mountain resort.

But now I know those were not the culprits. How do I know? I know because I have, at times in my own life, looked into the mirror and seen that same face. It is a look of sadness with a small amount of humor. Maybe it comes from actually being amused that life could be so good and inside you could feel so bad.

I do not know what went through Robin's mind as he slipped the belt around his neck. One wonders if he thought about his family, his wife, and the millions of fans who loved his talents. Probably not. Depression has a way of turning its victim so totally inward that anything outside that black box becomes invisible.

The first time I wrote about depression (*The Dark Night of the Soul - 3/13/11*), I was amazed at the response. Emails flooded my office as people who had been in the shadows acknowledged their depression and decided to let a little light in. Later blogs on depression led to the same flood of responses. It was obvious this subject had hit a nerve.

In a later posting, I explained the difference between chemical and/ or environmental depression as I defined them. Based on the feedback from that post, I learned that hundreds of people went to the doctor only to find out their depression could be controlled. In my case, it is controlled by one little pill I take each morning. For others with chemical depression, perhaps it is two pills, but the point is that there is an answer.

Others who were seeking answers wrote of seeking help from mental help professionals. In my experience, just acknowledging the symptoms was enough to get me moving in the right direction.

But from whatever direction this killer approaches its victim, there is a way to fight back. If you are trying to define the stalker in your own circumstances you might want to go to The Depression Center as a starting point.

I do not know the source of Robin's depression, but it ultimately took his life for whatever reason. I have watched this killer stalk so many of my friends. It did not surprise me that the killer would stalk and ultimately kill one of my favorite entertainers.

In life, this very funny man shared many life lessons with us. But if he could have one more day, I think he would have encouraged those of us with this disease to tell someone. To get help immediately. Perhaps he would have said, "It's OK. A lot of us suffer, but there is help to be had. This bastard got me, but it doesn't have to get you."

And yet the cynical among us would say, "Yea, but if he was such a hot shot, why did he kill himself?"

As we contemplate his answer to that question, my answer to Robin would be that wonderful line from the film *Good Will Hunting*. He is looking into the face of a young student when he says

"Look at me, Son. It's not your fault."

Finally, holding this young man in his arms, he says it four more times.

"Look at me, Son. It's not your fault."
"Look at me, Son. It's not your fault."
"Look at me, Son. It's not your fault."
"It's not your fault"

Robin, you suffered, and ultimately you lost the battle. But before you died, you brought a lot of joy into this troubled world. Yes, one lonely day when the darkness was too great, the killer got you. But

"Look at me, Son. It's not your fault."
The Suicide Hot Line - 1-800-273-TALK

CHAPTER THIRTY-ONE

We seem to be coming to the last chapter of our journey together. We started this journey with a smashed cat and hope to end on a much more serious note. At the original posting of the "smashed cat" blog, a reader sent me a text asking if that story was true.

After reading the republished smashed cat story, it seems wise to address the question before it arises again. To be clear, may I ask you:

If Pigs Could Talk

Don't you think they would tell the same "smashed cat" story?

Case made and closed.

Changing the subject, have you ever thought about the significance of coming to "The End" of various subjects or categories of your life? For instance, "All in the Family" was one of my favorite TV series. Launched in 1971, the bigoted life of Archie Bunker filled the airways for nine seasons. Who can forget his airhead wife, Edith, or his black neighbor, George Jefferson?

The final episode of "All in the Family" was broadcast on April 8, 1979. At our house, we had a "Bye, bye Archie" party where we pulled up the chairs into theater style. Our neighbors were black, white, Indian (with a dot, not an arrow), and everything in between. I distinctly remember my black neighbor three houses down coming to the party. He came up behind me and threw his arm around me. I flinched and turned red when Harry laughingly commented, "Caught you in an Archie moment, didn't I?"

As we both got a laugh from his comment, I was reminded of the "All in the Family " theme song, "Those Were the Days." And, indeed, those were the days. Harry didn't sue me because I still had some Arkansas mud between my toes, and I didn't burn a cross in his yard to make some bigoted point.

But then the credits began to roll, and there it was,

coming across the screen as big as my eighteen-inch, black-and-white TV could display

THE END

It was over. The last episode ended. Those two words said it all.

As I have previously confessed, I went to Baylor on an English scholarship and proceeded to flunk freshman English four times. There is a story behind this "dumbest student in the class" tragedy, but I will just hit the highlights. My favorite teacher of all time was Mrs. Caldwell, my High School English teacher. Her husband was the Superintendent of the school, and together they were a tough pair.

Mr. Caldwell had a permanent frown, and only once in all my high school years did I see him smile. In my Junior year, there came a week when Mr. Caldwell was to be in Little Rock for a conference of some type. It was announced in the school paper that Mr. C would not be in his office the following week.

Never wanting an opportunity like this to pass unnoticed, I decided to become Superintendent for the week. So every time I had a study period, I would go to Mr. C's office instead of going to the library and sitting at his desk I would do my homework. No one questioned me, so by Thursday, I was becoming rather bold in my impersonation of Mr. C. At that point, I decided to step it up a notch.

Mr. C's secretary was Mary Riddle. Mary had been out of High School for only a year when Mr. C employed her as his full-time secretary. Mary and I were friends from grade school. She was cute, friendly, knowledgeable about my mischievous nature, and always willing to be my partner in crime.

So I suggested that, since by Thursday, no one had called the police on me for using Mr. C's office, perhaps it was time to have Mary come in and sit on my lap. I told her I wanted to really see what it was like to be the Big Man.

Mary was about four inches taller than me, but the rest of the world was also taller than me. Mary, to obtain that height advantage, had the longest legs of any girl in town. The package was topped off by deep baby blue eyes, a smile that would break the mirror, and other attributes that I will not describe at this time. Let it be said that I was a bit smitten by Mary Legs. Oops, sorry, Mary Riddle.

Assuming Mary would be a willing partner in crime, I suggested that I sit at Mr. C's desk. Mary then suggested it might be more realistic if she came over and sat on my lap. Agreeing with the proposed seating arrangement, Mary proceeded to unwrap those long legs as she sat on my lap, facing me with her arms around my neck.

Do you have the picture firmly embedded in your mind? Well, so did Mr. C. It seems his conference was over on Wednesday, and now on Thursday, here he is, standing at the door to his office with the previously described scene firmly fixed in his brain.

Need I say more?

So why did you flunk Freshman English four times at Baylor?

Seriously, after that great story, do you really think anyone cares?

THE END

I think we could all agree that those two words have a special meaning in the American lexicon. *The End.* It is over. There is nothing more to be said.

Archie had no more episodes in which to entertain us. I had no need to take Freshman English again. It was over. I had no need to continue the embarrassment and humiliation any longer. I had reached "The End" of those events in my life.

Now I would like to give you a few facts about my current "dot" on the timeline of life. I am writing the first draft of this final chapter on May 6, 2023. As of today, I am approximately five months into my 83rd year of life. As of the sunrise this morning, I have already lived 30,575 days. According to insurance actuarial tables, I am likely to live nine more years.

Ah, but let me throw a few additional facts into the equation. Since 1900 no male in the Gill genetic line, of which I am one, has ever lived past 55 years of age, with three exceptions. Uncle Red died at 63 but lived the last 12 years of his life in a deep coma. For all practical purposes, he died at 51.

I had a cousin who, I believe, died at 61. And then there is old Ben Gill, who sits here at 83 with few health problems and still able to sit on the floor and stand up without using my hands for support. So this old boy is trucking right along.

But the fact still remains that in the course of my lifetime, I am not too far from

The End

About two years ago, I started meeting with about 10 or 12 guys every Tuesday morning to just talk about life together. When asked by an outsider what we do in our meetings, we just say, "Oh, I'm just meeting with a few guys who have decided to do life together." Isn't that simple? We are just a group of guys who have decided to do life together.

Sometimes a member of the group might share something deeply personal. Perhaps they want to talk about an aging parent, or their company is having financial problems, and they just need a private place to talk about their concerns.

Maybe they have lost their job and just need a bit of encouragement. As confidence has grown in the group, guys have come to know that there is a place where no one is going to "rat me out." This is a place where guys have come to love me enough to help me get through the hard times of life.

You know, as guys, we have a hard time with that. Guys are not used to talking about the hard things in life. But it is nice when we know we have a place to land if we are about to fall.

I am the oldest member of the group I attend, so I get a lot of questions about old people stuff. A few weeks ago, one member asked me, "Why do you think you get so many questions about dying? Do you think it is because you are so close to the end?"

My answer surprised him. I said, "No, I think it is because I have learned a way to beat the game. I have learned a way to win over death, and, as a result, *"The End"* is actually *"The Beginning."*

There is a guy in the Old Testament named Job. He asked one of the most significant questions a person will ever ask. His question,

"If a man dies, shall he live again?"

Since the beginning of humankind, people have attempted to answer that question. And only one man gives the answer they are seeking, and that man is the central figure of the Bible.

Now, it is at this point that someone says, "Oh, the Bible. I thought we were going to stay from fiction." This is usually followed by raucous laughter.

Consider these comments for a moment.

1. **Have you ever heard of Bethlehem?** You probably said, "Yes, that is where Jesus was born, and we sing about it every Christmas." But why would you know that? At the time of Jesus' birth, Bethlehem was just a tiny village about five miles from Jerusalem. And yet, you know of that village because Jesus was born there.

2. **Ever heard of Nazareth?** Jesus grew up there. About five years ago, Holly and I visited this little town of about 700 people. We only know about Nazareth because Jesus grew up there as a kid.

3. **Do you have a calendar?** Do you know why it is divided up into BC and AD? The calendar of the Universe is divided that way because Jesus' birth separates the division of dates - BC - before Christ.

4. **Think about this.** You are acknowledging the importance of Jesus every time you look at your iPhone. Apple engineers put the date on the home screen. So you see the date, which was established according to the birth of Jesus.

5. **Here is a good one.** To be considered for the New York Times best-seller list, you must have a minimum of 5,000 book sales.

   The British Book Publishing Society estimates that between 5-7,000,000,000 (that's BILLION) copies of the Bible have been printed and sold. That book's central character is Jesus. Maybe that is why you have heard of Him.

   The Bible is a library of sixty-six books written by 35 different authors over the course of several hundred years. Maybe that is why the name of Jesus sounds so familiar.

6. **Now, are you ready to get very specific?** Isaiah was a Prophet who lived approximately 850 years before Christ was born. But Isaiah wrote,

"Therefore, the Lord himself will give you a sign. Behold, the virgin shall conceive and bear a son and shall call his name Immanuel."

Isaiah 7:14

Isaiah wrote these words 850 years before Jesus' birth. "Behold, the virgin..."

The Bible, a book that has sold between 5-7 billion copies, says that Jesus will be born of a virgin. He will be called Immanuel, which means "God with us."

As the church grew, a great follower of Jesus named Paul, known as Paul the Apostle or Saint Paul, wrote a letter to the early church in Rome. In the Bible, that book is simply called *Romans.* In that book, a series of statements will lead us to the answer to our question.

Paul writes, "**For all have sinned and come short of the glory of God.**" *Romans* **3:23** It is our nature to sin, and Paul says we have all committed sin. I don't know about you, but I can't argue with that statement.

Now what is the penalty for sin? Again, in **Romans 6:23**, Paul writes to this new church the following: *For the wages of sin is death, but the gift of God is eternal life through Jesus Christ our Lord.* As I read that, I get the idea that there is not a lot of wiggle room in Paul's statement.

Let's move on.

Then Paul offers a statement of hope. "*But the gift of God is ETERNAL LIFE through Jesus Christ our Lord.*" *Romans* **6:23**

Just a sentence or two later, Paul continues, "*But God demonstrates His own love toward us, in that while we were still sinners, Christ died for us."* Make sure you get the sequence right. First, we have sinned. Second, the penalty for our sins is death. Third, since the penalty had to be paid by someone, Jesus stepped up and said, "I will pay the penalty for (insert your name). I will die for that person."

So in an eternal sacrifice to pay off our debt, Jesus died on the cross for us.

And finally, Paul says, "Just do this and accept that Jesus paid for your sin. *"If you will confess with your mouth, Jesus as Lord, and believe in your heart that God raised Him from the dead, you will be saved."*

What was Job's question? "If a man dies, shall he live again?"

Now we are back to the beginning, where Paul writes to this early church to affirm, *"But the gift of God is eternal life through Jesus Christ our Lord."*

So Job, do you have the answer to your question? I thought so. I am glad we could help you out. But now, each of us needs to ask the same question.

"If I die, will I live again?"

Most of us get hung up at this point because we think we need to get all religious and approach God with a lot of "thees and thou" sort of words. Why don't you just stop right now and talk to God like you would talk to your best friend?

Maybe just say this prayer with me.

"Jesus, this is (insert your first name) just coming to talk with you. Jesus, I know I have sinned against you, and I know that I deserve to die for those sins. Jesus, I was reading a book today that said if I would confess to you that I am sorry for being a sinner and if I would accept the fact that you paid my death penalty by dying on the cross for me, you would forgive me.

Jesus, I know you died in my place, and I trust you for salvation. Lord, please forgive me of my sins, and I ask you to come into my life.

Amen.

Now, think of someone whom you know will be happy about your decision to accept Christ into your heart. Maybe it is your Mom or Dad, a close friend, or a person at work whom you know is a Christian.

Even though it is a BIG deal, don't make a big

deal out of telling someone. Just say something like this, "I know you are a Christian, and I want you to be one of the first to know that I have put my trust in Jesus too."

Do you know what is going to happen? You are going to find that by taking this first step, you will soon realize you are not facing

The End

you have just found

THE BEGINNING

The End

Of this book, but

The Beginning of Your Life

About the Author

Ben Gill was the Founder and CEO of the largest fundraising organization in the world. The organization, RSI/ Viscern, was based in Dallas, TX, where Ben and his wife, Holly, lived until his retirement in 2005.

Ben is an internationally known humourist, convention speaker, and writer. Over the years, his hobbies have included golf, writing, jumping out of perfectly good airplanes, surviving bike crashes, and just bumming around, making a nuisance of himself.

Devoted Christians, the Gills attend The Vail Church in Avon, CO.

Since 2016 the Gills have resided full-time in Edwards, CO.

Made in the USA
Las Vegas, NV
10 November 2023